W
Take Two

Telcine Turner

MACMILLAN
CARIBBEAN

Characters

Harold Davies	45.	Up-and-coming businessman concerned with saving face.
Erma Davies	40.	Harold's wife who has not kept up with him.
Matilda Bascombe		Maid to the **Davies** family. Mainly a catalyst.
Sonia Davies		Sixteen going on blithely.
Beverly Humes		19 and determined
Merline Evans	50.	Perhaps overly-conscious of her duties to Beverly.
Jennifer Evans		Daughter to **Merline**, aged 10 years.
Lionel Joseph	20.	Employed by **Harold Davies**. Son of a Haitian immigrant.
Young Lady		Applicant for the **Davies'** job.
Five Children		Three boys, two girls, to play ring-play with **Jennifer**.

Setting

New Providence Island in the pre-independent Bahamas of the early 1970s.

ACT ONE

Scene 1.

A Friday morning in January in the Davies living-room

The room is tastefully furnished with a sofa, two matching chairs, and a liquor cabinet. On a telephone stand are a bunch of keys, a wallet, and a chequebook. **Harold Davies**, *middle-aged and attractive, enters, wearing tailored slacks, a long-sleeved shirt, and socks. He searches for his shoes and finds them under the sofa. As he begins putting them on* **Erma Davies** *enters, wearing a housecoat and slippers. She still retains some of the good looks she possessed in her youth, despite much childbearing.*

Erma: I thought you would try to sneak off without even eating breakfast.

Harold: I was not sneaking off. [*Finishes tying his laces.*] Where is my briefcase?

Erma: Just where you left it—in some woman's closet. I want to know where you been all night last night.

Harold: Celebrating with one of the fellows.

Erma: What was her name?

Harold: *His* wife just had a son. Something you never quite managed. [*Exits and returns with his tie, coat, and a briefcase, into which he stuffs the wallet and chequebook. Takes up the keys*] See you. [*Kisses* **Erma***'s cheeks.*]

Erma: Harold, stay home tonight longer than it take to change your clothes. Talk to me, to the children.

Harold: Tonight I'm going to Miami. On business.

Erma: What business? Same thing I was saying . . . which one it is this time? Lucille?

Harold: Stop sounding so loose. [*Turns to leave.*]

Erma: I'm going with you. [*Snatches* **Harold**'*s sleeve. He pushes her off.*]

Harold: Your place is in my house with my children, not snooping around business deals. Get that into your head.

Erma: That last trip to New York was supposed to be business, too, but your secretary went 'long.

Harold: It *was* business. Look, Erma, why don't you wake up? I'd never get anywhere if all I thought about was laying every woman in sight. [*Pats her hip.*] Come to think of it, mightn't be such a bad idea . . . Your trouble is boredom. Another baby would cure that.

Erma: Baby! Baby! Think of me for a change, not just babies.

Harold: Apologies. See you. [*Heads for the exit, but stops when* **Erma** *calls.*]

Erma: Harold? Sonia home all day; she need something to do. Take her to the office with you.

Harold: You trying to spy on me? [*Silence.*] All right. [*Goes out and comes across* **Matilda** *listening outside.*] What you doing out here?

Matilda: Oh, good mornin, Mr. Davies. I just wanted to see the missis.

[**Harold** *leaves.* **Matilda** *enters, tall, lean, long-necked, wearing a maid's uniform and low-heeled black shoes. Her habitual manner implies to whoever she is with that she knows a secret nobody else does.* **Erma** *eyes her with mistrust.*]

Matilda: Mornin, Missis Davies. How you is this bright-sun mornin?

Erma: No sun shinin in here. Matilda, why you stand outside?

Matilda: Mr. Davies was here, and you tell me not to come in when the two o' yawl inside.

Erma: I tell you not to come in without knocking, since too often you just "happened" to barge in when we discussin private family matters. I didn't say skulk outside.

Matilda [*Putting on a self-righteous air*]: I might be poor—that ain' no sin. Plenty others start out the same way. But I don't skulk. I don't gat that kind of evil mind . . . Something I had was to tell you, Ma'am.

Sonia *pokes her head in.*

Sonia: 'Bye, Mother. [*Exits. Door slams.*]

Erma: The girls being sassy?

Matilda: No, ma'am. Ma'am, I don' know quite how to put this . . .

Erma: Put what? I will not listen to gossip 'bout my husband.

Matilda *looks smug, as though a theory of hers has proven correct.*

Matilda: 'Tain' gossip and don' concern Mr. Davies. Ma'am, I would be the last to come between man and wife . . . "What God hath joined together let no man put asunder!" No, ma'am, is Miss Sonia . . . I can' say for sure what the matter partic'lar is with her, but dese hero-o-lates when I fix bacon and egg for breakfast she does leave hers.

Erma: Nothing wrong with that. She probably don't like it.
Matilda: She did before.
Erma: People change.
Matilda: Not with dey favourite food . . . Maybe is der grease.
Erma: Nonsense. Examination nerves. Those exams coming up in June.
Matilda: Only January now. By time is June, ma'am, you'll have ghost on hand . . . [*Helpfully*] Maybe you should take her to doctor.
Erma: Sonia is as healthy as a horse.
Matilda: Plenty sick horse round dis Nassau Town, and I never yet hear 'bout horse throwing up.

Erma *shows her alarm.*

Erma: Sonia threw up? When?
Matilda: No later than dis mornin. She fly past me like hurricane to reach der bathroom. Aye, aye, when I get dere, dere she was, bendin over the facebowl, bringin up what she ain' even eat . . . It been goin' on all dis week, ma'am.
Erma: How come I never notice?
Matilda: Beg your pardon, Ma'am, but look to me like you was occupy wid other things . . . Now me, I notice. I notice. After all, das what you pay me for. Is my duty.
Erma: Thanks for letting me know, Matilda.
Matilda: Maybe you should call doctor now, Ma'am. [*Looks encouragingly from* **Erma** *to the telephone. Awkward silence.*] Mustn't forget doctor appointment . . . I mean, so much people in doctor office dese days you gotta wait, even *with* appointment. *Without* is worse . . . You want I should tidy up in here now?

Erma *looks as though her mind is a ways off.*

Matilda: I could tidy here now?
Erma [*Coming to herself*]: What? Er . . . yes. Might as well.

Matilda *goes out.* **Erma** *paces downstage, her right hand straying repeatedly to her neck.*

Erma: No, can't be. Not Sonia. She can't be makin the same mistake I make. [*Thinks.*] Maybe I should call the office. Talk to her . . . No. No cause for fright. Mustn't let it worry me. After all, probably is a simple explanation for all this. Not to worry. Keep calm. Must keep calm.

Erma *exits upstage as if in a daze. Slow fade.*

ACT ONE

Scene 2. Later the same morning in Merline's combination front/dining-room

The room is simply furnished with a small sofa and matching armchair, a little table with a gaudy electric lamp and a radio, and a vinyl dinette set. **Beverly** *is curled up in the armchair, reading a magazine. From backstage right come voices of five children and* **Jennifer** *raised in anticipation of a ring-play game. They rush in and converge in a circle downstage, in front of the room.* **Beverly** *lays aside the book to watch.*

Children [*Clapping and singing*]:
Blue Hill water dry;
No way to wash my clothes.
I remember the Saturday night,
Boiled fish and johnny cake.

(*Chant*) Man take one and satisfy;
Woman take two and make a moo!*
Man take one and satisfy;
Woman take two and make a moo!

Jennifer *ends her dance by gyrating in front of a boy. She rejoins the others on the circumference of the circle while the boy dances inside the ring as they all clap and repeat the formula.*

Children:
Blue Hill water dry;
No way to wash my clothes.

*Bahamian dialect for "move."

I remember the Saturday night,
Boiled fish and johnny cake.

(*Chant*) Man take one and satisfy;
Woman take two and make a moo!
Man take one and satisfy;
Woman take two and make a moo!

Merline *parts the curtains at the upstage end of her front room and watches the children indignantly. She is slow-moving and portly, wears a house-dress and scarf, and carries a thick leather belt in her right hand. She advances to the doorway.*

Merline: Well, by damn! Big Friday mornin and dis all yinna could find to do? Every one a yawl go where you belong. Make noise in yer own ma head!

The children scatter. **Jennifer** *mounts the wooden steps leading into the room fearfully and tries to edge past her mother.* **Merline***'s hand flashes out and the belt slaps across* **Jennifer***'s back. The girl dashes through the curtains.*

Merline: I don' know what to do with her. Almost twelve years and all she wan' do is dance dem vulgar ring-play dance.

Beverly: Sounds like you never played jump-in dance when you were small. Let her have her fun; after all, today is her school's holiday. You don't have to beat her for everything.

Merline: Look like you wan' tell me how to raise my one child. The Lord give me Jennifer when I did lost hope of having any children. He mussie know what He was doin'. Since He put her in my care I goin' do my best to bring her up right . . . Right now she is more woman than I was at her age.

Beverly: Things are different now.

Merline: *Too* different. What we did know about love magazines and fingernail polish?

Beverly: Auntie Merl, if you have something to say please come out and say it. If you don't like my nail polish and magazines say so one time, instead of spelling and spelling.

Merline: Jennifer wan' do everything you do. Is always "Beverly this" and "Beverly that." If it stopped dere I wouldn' mind, but now she wan' dress like you. Wouldn' be surprise if she does read them love books you gat all over der place.

Beverly: They don't have anything bad in them. She might as well read *something.*

Merline: No, thanks. Trash goin' give her ideas. Time enough for dat when she grown . . . And, miss lady, instead of laying here like the queen of Sheba you should be out lookin for job. The li'l money I get cleanin people clothes don' go far, and the money you give me from yer last job just about gone . . . Yer save any?

Beverly: No. I gave it to Lionel.

Merline: You do what?

Beverly: As down payment on our lot. It was only eight hundred dollars.

Merline: You gat your right sense, girl? One dollar is fortune for the man what broke . . . No wonder he been comin 'round here so regular.

Beverly: Now, Auntie Merl . . .

Merline: Look. Gettin' engaged to dat Lion-el was your idea, but even if you fool enough to throw yourself away on a half-Haitian . . .

Beverly: He's not half anything! He was born here just like you and me. He is *all* Bahamian, *all* man, and *all* mine! You don't have to like him; after all, it's me he's marrying, not you. But the least you could do is stop downgrading him every chance you get!

Merline: Lord, gimme faith! To have a li'l gal scarce out the eggshell talkin to me any which way . . . Get this, Bev'ly, and get it good: I never had chance for fancy edgecation like yinna so, but what I done forget yawl will never even learn . . . Dis my house. It might not look like much to proper-speakin' people like you, with dey heart set on mansion, but is mine! Mine! And don' forget dat. [**Beverly** *turns her back to* **Merline**.] Don' turn way; hear me out . . . If I say dat thin-chest, scrawny-neck, piss-tail boy you pick up back o' der bush is half-Haitian, he's half-Haitian! [**Beverly** *moves towards the front steps.*] Walk outa here while I talkin' and you might as well don' come back . . . And to think. To think how I went outa my way to oblige yer ma when she send you down here to school. How I feed you, shelter you, and clothes you. And dis is the tanks I get. I could treat you like my own child, but I mustn't mention yer friends.

Beverly: It isn't just mentioning. You always pick on Lionel just because his daddy came from Haiti.

Merline: He coulda come from Jerusalem for all I care. Das but a part of it. [**Beverly** *looks at her.*] Der young man worthless in he own right.

Beverly: How you could say that? What he ever do to you?

Merline: You blind, but I can see.

Beverly: See what?

Merline: Ent he take your money? Das der first sign.

Beverly: Sign?

Merline: Of worthlessness. Any man so hurry to take money from a woman before dey married gatta be worthless!

Beverly: The lot is mine as well as his.

Merline: Not till you say "I do." When your Uncle Ephraim—God rest the dead—ask me to marry him, he already had house build. I didn't have to put a cent, not one single, solitary cent . . . You ever stop to think what would happen to your money if you two was to break up?

Beverly: After all this time? That won't happen.

Silence. **Merline** *is casting around for a way to warn* **Beverly**. *She is about to resort to traditional proverbial sayings.* **Beverly** *will attempt to convince herself that her aunt's suspicions are without foundation; the younger woman's answers should give the impression that she is talking to herself, almost.*

Merline: Never take a leaky bucket to der well.

Beverly: No way.

Merline: Old people say . . .

Beverly: Don't have to worry 'bout that.

Merline: T'ree things come not back . . .

Beverly: Won't give Lionel up . . .

Merline: Der word, once said . . .

Beverly: . . . for anyone else.

Merline: . . . de arrow dat is sped . . .

Beverly: And he feels the same about me.

Merline: . . . and lost opportunity. [*Sighs. Prepares to go. Looks at* **Beverly**.] Well, you gone this far might as well go further. Secure yourself. When he come make him name the wedding day. [*Silence.*] Sun high. I goin' get somethin ready to eat.

Merline *goes out. Lights go down on* **Beverly** *as she sits, thinking, on the front doorstep.*

ACT ONE

Scene 3. Later that morning in Harold Davies's outer office

Furniture is utilitarian. Lights come up on **Sonia** *talking on the telephone.*

Sonia: I'm calling because I have to, that's why . . . Let them hear . . . No, I didn't do what you suggested, for reasons of my own . . . Hasn't it occurred to you that I might want him, whether you do or not? . . . I'm damaging your career? What you think you do to mine? I'm not crazy about going to college, but still . . . Your wife? What about my parents? News of this will kill Mother for sure, and Daddy will throw me out. Say I'm a needy constituent . . . You've got to go? Wait one cotton-pickin minute . . . [*Holds the receiver away from her ears a second then slams it down.*] Dirty skunk! [**Sonia** *stares in disgust at the telephone.* **Lionel** *enters from down left, enraged.*]

Lionel: Turning me round and round like some jackass!
Sonia: Beg your pardon?
Lionel: Mr. Davies in?
Sonia: No. Could I help?
Lionel: Yeah, if you can take resignations. Davies and Miller can take their two-bit job and stuff it! [*Walks up and down*] Treating me like some errand boy! Who the hell he think he is, ordering me around? Why, I know more about this job than he does, yet he orders me around. Shee-it!

Sonia: Mister, the least you could do is explain what put you in such a bad temper. And don't take it out on me, and don't curse in here. This is not a bar-room. It's the front office of Davies Construction Company. It's a place of business.

Lionel: And I mean business! Tell Davies to find someone else to work with Miller. I have had it up to here! [*Indicates his throat.*]

Sonia: Tell him yourself. I don't deal with personnel.

Lionel: When you expect him back?

Sonia: Any time before one. Please have a seat.

Lionel: Might as well. [*Sits.*]

Sonia: So what did Miller do?

Lionel: It's what he *didn't* do! Anyone knows when you start a job the supplies should be on hand. Well, Miller doesn't operate that way. First he orders only enough blocks to lay the foundation, and when I tell him that was a silly way to work he gets on his high horse. Now the foundation is laid and he still hasn't got in more blocks. I ask him how he expects a respectable mason to work under those conditions and you know what that animal said? That bunch of slime said I should be glad getting paid for doin' nothing and if I want blocks I could go for them myself or shut up. That's some gall, sending me to do his work!

Sonia: Why you complaining? You'll get paid, whatever Mr. Miller does.

Lionel: Yeah, I do the thinking and he gets the credit. Look, I can't stand sloppiness, especially in someone supposed to be over me. When I go on a job I go to work. Let the supplies be there, talk to me decent, or no dice.

Sonia: You can't always have it your way.

Lionel: Why not, if it's the best way?

Sonia: Full of yourself, aren't you?

Lionel: No other way to be . . . [*Offers her a cigarette*] Try to reason with that bald-headed fool. [*Lights the cigarettes.*]

Sonia: Thanks; this can't make me feel worse.

Lionel: You sick? Sorry. Hope I didn't cause it, sounding off like that.

Sonia: No. I left home feeling bad.

Lionel: You should've stayed there and let old Davies mind his own shop for one day.

Sonia: It's pleasanter here and "old Davies" could use the help.

Lionel: What happened to the other girl?

Sonia: Lucille?

Lionel: Must be her.

Sonia: You work for this company and don't know the secretary's name?

Lionel: Too much trouble. Look, I no sooner get to learn their names than they up and leave, then I have to unlearn what I learned and start all over again. Waste of brainpower. [*Leans forward confidentially*] Would you believe in the past sixteen months no less than five girls have sat behind that desk? [*Holds up five fingers*] Five. Must be a disease around here.

Sonia: A disease named Davies . . . "Old Davies" is my daddy. I'm the oldest of five.

Lionel: He was a busy man.

Sonia: Still is. Guess he can't help it, though. That's the way men are.

Lionel: You women don't exactly make it hard for us, if you know what I mean.

Sonia: That the voice of experience?

Lionel: Don't get me wrong. I'm not looking. I've got mine.

Sonia: Never roached on her?

Lionel: Never needed to.
Sonia: Or temptation wasn't strong enough? [*Stares at him. He returns her stare.*]
Lionel: If I didn't know better I'd get ideas about you; about where you're headed. [*Stands and paces restlessly.*]
Sonia: Where am I headed?
Lionel: Never mind . . . I hate waiting 'round offices. Is a waste of time and boring.
Sonia: Back to business . . . What did Mr. Miller send you for? [*Sees* **Lionel's** *annoyance.*] I mean, what did *you* come for? I take it you're still working for us?

Lionel *laughs;* **Sonia** *follows his example.*

Lionel: I need a purchase order for bricks from Claridge. Make it double the amount we got last time and let me get out of here. The job is Carey—T. Carey, Stapledon Gardens.

Sonia *riffles through a file on the desk.*

Sonia: Carey . . . Cable Beach, Cara Associates, Carder, Cardone . . . Like I was saying . . .
Lionel [*Caught unawares*]**:** What?
Sonia: Daddy's weakness is women; Mother's is high blood pressure. The two don't go together, I can tell you. One of these times when she finds out about him and his latest triumph, that will be the end of the line for her.
Lionel: How does she find out?
Sonia: Whenever he goes on a business trip and takes his secretary. Mind, he always has an explanation, but Mother's up to his tricks by now. Mister, if you don't mind, I have work to do.

Lionel *laughs.*

Lionel: You really are something . . . How old are you anyway?

Sonia: Sixteen.

Lionel: Sixteen going on a hundred.

Sonia: Honest, I'm sixteen. I'll be seventeen in June. I'm Gemini. [*Recites*] "You are a quick and intelligent thinker. People find you congenial for your excellent sense of humour. You are inclined to expect too much for too little and should learn to work persistently to achieve the success of which you are capable . . . " Not bad, hey?

Lionel: You believe that stuff?

Sonia: At least the part about being lazy. You know, if I wanted to I could be a genius. No funning. Last year I sat seven GCEs and passed five with credit. Failed math and English, but I signed up to take them at GHS Evening Institute.

Lionel: Sounds like a good idea. I'll check that out tonight.

Sonia: Not that I look forward to any more classes.

Lionel: Born with a silver spoon in your mouth and you spit it out.

Sonia: Silver spoon nothing! Wait 'til someone tells you how to run your life; see if you'll like it . . . Funny. Here we are chatting like old enemies and I don't even know your name. What is it?

Lionel: Lionel Joseph.

Silence.

Sonia: Lionel Joseph what? That's all?

Lionel: That—as you say—is all. But one day my name is going to mean something. I'm proud as hell of Joseph.

Sonia [*Embarrassed*]: It's got strength.
Lionel: I come from strong people.
Sonia [*Trying to change the trend of the conversation*]: And you're a mason . . . You sure don't sound like one.

Silence. **Lionel** *glares at* **Sonia**.

Lionel: How should a mason sound?
Sonia: Put my foot in my mouth again, hey?
Lionel: Forget it. How are you to know that not everyone who matches y-o-u with a-r-e pushes a pen in some office? I'm a mason, but a mason with a plan. I'm not going to bow and scrape and run errands for no shit like Miller all the days of my life, no sirree! [*Strides around, hands behind his back.*] Not me. I've got dreams. I'll be the boss: no more "please, sirs" and "thank yous." I'll wave my hand and see condominiums spring from Abaco to Inagua . . . I'll be glorious as the poinciana.
Sonia: Some dream.
Lionel: I'll make it true.
Sonia: Easy as it seems?
Lionel: First plan, then do [*Sings*]

It's best to be your own boss
And do exactly what you want to do.
It's best to be your own boss—
To sleep and get up when you want to . . .

Stops. Realises where he is.

Got carried away there, didn't I?
Sonia: Who's complaining? Any more?

Lionel *sings the verses with zest.* **Sonia** *joins in the chorus hesitantly, then with increasing confidence.*

Lionel:

Round here we have some people
Who can't tell where they are.
Every time you look they're movin,
Yet they don't get very far.
Strainin out their guts
For somebody else
When they could be workin for themselves!

[*Chorus*]

It's best to be your own boss
And do exactly what you want to do.
It's best to be your own boss—
To sleep and get up when you want to.

I knew a li'l old lady,
With a face all full of smiles,
Used to work for some rich people
And had to walk for miles.
In the heat and the rain
She toiled forty years, alone;
When her mortgage lapsed, that didn't save
her home.

It's best to be your own boss
And do exactly what you want to do.
It's best to be your own boss—
To sleep and get up when you want to.

During the singing of the last stanza **Harold Davies** *enters down left and watches.* **Sonia** *sees him, stops singing and completes the purchase order.* **Lionel** *hears the silence and turns around to face* **Harold** *uneasily.*

Harold: This what I pay you for? Entertainment?

Lionel: Sir, you can't expect me to work without material. I came for an order to get more blocks. Mr. Miller sent me.

Harold: So why didn't you get the order and go, instead of hanging 'round here like it is The Three Queens?

Sonia: But Daddy, you said not to sign anything in your absence, to tell them to wait.

Sonia *hands* **Harold** *the order. He signs it and gives it to* **Lionel.**

Harold: I forgot. Too many things to think about . . . How's the job coming, Joseph?

Lionel: All right, sir. But I wish I didn't have to work with Mr. Miller. He doesn't know how to talk to people.

Harold: His bark's worse than his bite. I'll drop by this afternoon and have a talk with him . . . Get them to deliver the stuff. We don't want to overwork our trucks.

Lionel: Yes, sir.

Lionel *leaves.* **Harold** *turns wrathfully on* **Sonia**.

Harold: You should know better than to carouse with a common worker.

Sonia: We were not carousing, and Lionel is not common. People like you and Mr. Miller try to make out that he is, but one of these days he'll surprise you. He'll give you competition. He as much as said so.

Harold: Biggity!* That's those Haitians for you. Stay away from him. Just to make sure, look in the files and phone in that secretary ad to the *Tribune* for tonight.

Sonia: Yes, sir.

Harold *retreats through the door marked Private.* **Sonia** *extracts an ad copy from a file and dials a number on the telephone.*

Sonia: Hello, the *Tribune*? . . . I want to place an ad for this evening's paper, please . . . Yes. [*Waits. Speaks slowly and distinctly*] "Wanted: efficient secretary, Davies Construction Company . . . "

Lights fade.

*Bahamian dialect for "bigoted."

ACT ONE

Scene 4. Lunch-time, the same day, in Merline's front room

Beverly *lies on the floor reading a magazine and facing the frontyard.* **Jennifer** *appears up right, lugging an ironing-board; she leans the board against the dining-table.*

Beverly: Where you going with that?
Jennifer: Mama tell me to bring it in here.
Beverly: Since when do we iron in the front room?
Jennifer: Maybe one o' Mama friends comin and dey want talk.
Beverly: But Auntie knows this the time Lionel stops by on his way to lunch . . . Help me pretty up in here. Get some hibiscus for the table.

Jennifer *runs off, down right.* **Beverly** *dusts furniture with tissue and straightens doilies and cushions.* **Jennifer** *re-enters with hibiscus in a jar.*

Beverly: I'll go freshen up. Get out the yard broom and sweep in the front. And if Lionel comes talk to him till I come. And if Auntie shows up call me right away. Okay?

Beverly *goes out.* **Jennifer** *fetches a straw broom from backstage, but tosses it aside when she hears* **Lionel** *whistling "It's Best to Be Your Own Boss".*

Lionel: Hey there, princess! Up you go! [*He swings* **Jennifer** *off her feet.*] Get any heavier and I won't be able to do this . . . Beverly home?

Jennifer: In the house. She say I must talk to you 'til she get ready. [*Leads him to a chair.*] You sit there and I'll sit here. [*Sits.*]

Lionel: Who is ironing?

Jennifer: Mama, so she can talk to you, because she vexed with Bev . . . What we should talk 'bout?

Lionel: What do you want to talk about?

Jennifer: About me! Ask me what I want to be.

Lionel: Miss Evans, what do you want to be?

Jennifer [*Giggling*]**:** A dope addict! So I could get my picture in the papers. They always have pictures of people who use dope in the newspapers.

Lionel [*Laughing*]**:** Along with policemen! Try modelling or being an airline stewardess. They safer.

Jennifer: Know what I really want to be?

Lionel: What?

Jennifer: A secretary, like Bev.

Beverly *enters.*

Beverly: I heard my name. [*To* **Lionel**] How was Jen-Jen as a hostess?

Lionel: Top-rate.

Beverly: Thanks, Jen-Jen. One more favour. I'll need my black shoes for job-hunting Monday. You could polish them for me? When I "m" you can "d" to my "w."

Jennifer *exits, giggling.* **Beverly** *kisses* **Lionel.**

Lionel: Hi, sweets. How're you feeling?

Beverly: Rotten, like a prisoner in here. No job, no money, no place to go, having to put up all day with Auntie's nagging.

Lionel: You should be used to her by now.

Beverly: Lionel, you don't get used to a headache; you just wish it would go away.

Lionel: Or take medicine. [*Cuddles her.*] I'll be your aspirin and ease your headache . . . Let's go for a drive to South Beach, away from nagging aunts and prying eyes. My car is like a house.

Beverly: That's only temporary: I want permanent privacy!

Lionel: Bev, you let people get you down too easy. The worst thing you can do is give in under pressure. I came pretty close to wringing Miller's neck today, but I forced myself to calm down and forget about him.

Beverly: Then help me forget about Mama and Daddy and all those children on the island. Take me out tonight so I can forget.

Lionel: I can't. I'm going to class tonight.

Beverly: Since when?

Lionel: I signed up today.

Beverly: Then you can sign down tomorrow. What you need night classes for?

Lionel: To get ahead.

Beverly: You could get ahead without any piece of paper they could give you. You already have a drafting certificate from Technical. What more you need to be foreman?

Lionel: I want to be more than just a foreman. Bev, I want to start my own business, from small projects, after I finish the house.

Beverly: I see where you and me goin' fall out. Here I am in purgatory in this matchbox and you have money to waste on night classes. We could use that money to get married now. Two years ago we didn't have nothing and I said no to getting married. *Now* I say yes.

Lionel: We're young, Bev. We could wait till we finish the house.

Beverly: House! House! All you think of is house. For all I know I might drop dead tomorrow and you would take some other woman into the house. *Now,* Lionel. Weight broke down the wagon.

Merline [*Offstage*]: Beverly, you usin' the ironin board?

Beverly: No, Auntie.

Merline *appears.* **Lionel** *stands.*

Lionel: Afternoon, Mrs. Evans.

Merline: Afternoon, yourself. You don't work, hey? Seem like every time I turn round you somewhere underfoot.

Beverly: Auntie Merl, this is no time to talk lowness. Lionel is my guest.

Merline: Guest, hell! Dis ain' no hotel. [**Lionel** *moves toward the front exit.*] Not so fast. I want a word with you. In private.

Beverly: He came to see me. I'm the one who should be talking to him.

Merline: Your talkin don' accomplish shit. You want something to do, go fry dem goggle-eyes I season. Make yourself useful for a change.

Beverly *goes out.* **Merline** *sits in the armchair and regards* **Lionel** *steadily. He slowly sits down.* **Merline** *clasps her hands in her lap and looks at* **Lionel** *for a few moments in silence.*

Beverly [*Offstage*]: Jennifer, you finished my shoes?

Jennifer: One minute!

Silence.

Merline: Well, well, young man, what you have to say for yourself?

Lionel: How you mean, Mrs. Evans?

Merline: What is your intention?

Lionel: To live as long as God lets me, ma'am.

Merline [*Carefully*]**:** One mind tell me you tryin to crack joke at my expense. We ain' no company, remember dat. I here to lay my cards on der table and I wish you to do der same.

Lionel: No offence meant, Mrs. Evans, but I think what's between Beverly and me is for us to discuss, not anyone else. [*Rising*] So if you don't mind, I must be getting back to work, and . . .

Merline *eyes him calmly. He sits.*

Merline: Like I was sayin, we should lay our cards on der table . . . Me first . . . In my day, Mr. Joseph, young people did know 'bout love and courtship just like you all, but we had rules. A young man see a girl he like had to go to her parents or guardian and ask to visit the house. If and when they decide to get married he had to write der house to seek her hand. In der envelope with der letter he had to put de engagement ring. [**Lionel** *squirms on his chair.*] Patience. I say all that to say this: you young people today gat so much freeness it drunk you and make you crazy . . . Nowadays, a young man see a girl who look good to him, what he do? He talk to her direct and "make his play" as yinna call it—in public or on der sly. Den, if dey was to decide to get married der parents is der last to know, despite der fact that until children go on dey own dey is der parents' responsibility. Den if der man decide to move on, off he go; nothing to hold him back. Parents left with the damage and the piecin-back-togedder to do . . . Here is where I want to make my point: I ain' no scholar, but of this much I am sure: for all yinna big talk 'bout revolution and bein' free and doin' yer own ting, yawl ain' change human nature one bit from what it ever was. Yawl ain' make some people any less selfish or some others any less liable to get hurt. And whereas in my day der man was lawful bound to honour The Promise of der Ring and der Letter, now is scarcely ever ring and *never* letter. Is a shiftin mind and a slippery tongue what speak and leave nary a trace of what it say . . . I know you appreciate my concern for Beverly. I is her only real parents, and to me she is like a daughter . . . She ain' ugly and she ain' bad—much as she believe I think so . . .

Lionel: Yes, ma'am.

Merline: Well, considerin dat, answer me dis. You think is right to take Beverly hard-earn money and keep her hangin on to a promise made only with words? No ring, no letter, no certification, no security?

Lionel: Mrs. Evans, I get the point, but the truth is when we got engaged we decided to do without a ring and formality; and we didn't want to get married and start out with a struggle, without anything of our own.

Merline: You have something now. As for strugglin, only der dead don' struggle . . . Decide to get married and struggle together; otherwise bring back Beverly money. Go your way and let her go hers. What you say?

Lionel: I *do* want Beverly . . .

Merline: Heat o' the loins is not enough. For der good

times, maybe, but not der struggles. [*She stands; so does* **Lionel**.] For her you is a habit, and habits ain' easy to break, but is possible, so make up your mind. You can't give her back der past, but you can bring back her money . . . I done say my say. Is up to you. Understand?

Lionel: I understand. I'll think about it.

Merline: Do that.

Lionel: Er . . . tell Beverly I'll see her later, please.

Merline: How late is "later"?

Lionel: Can't say, ma'am.

Lionel *leaves without looking back.*

Merline: Beverly! Beverly, come here!

Beverly *enters.*

Merline: Lion-el say he will see you later.

Beverly: Auntie Merl, I hope you didn't insult him and make him leave.

Merline: Not a t'ing like it. I surprise myself, I act so civilize. [**Merline** *goes out.*]

Beverly: Jennifer! Jennifer, come help me!

Jennifer *enters.* **Beverly** *grabs her hand and leads her to the frontyard.*

Beverly: All right, say what you heard. Talk fast before Auntie looks out.

Jennifer: It sound like she was tellin Lionel . . .

Beverly: Don't tell me what it sounded like, just what she said.

Jennifer: First, she ask him bout his in . . . in . . .

Beverly: His intentions. Go on.

Jennifer: Then he say he wan' go, but he didn't go. After that she talk about courtin ship . . .

Beverly: Courtship. Go on.

Jennifer: . . . and about ring and letter . . .

Beverly: And after that?

Jennifer: Then Mama talk so much I almost fall 'sleep.

Beverly: What she say, Jen-Jen? Think.

Jennifer [*Slowly*]: About responsibility . . . and when she was a girl . . . and sand . . . and . . . and . . .

Beverly: Come, Jen-Jen.

Jennifer: Big words.

Beverly: Then?

Jennifer: She say you wasn't ugly, Bev! And about strugglin togedder.

Beverly: That's good. Any more?

Jennifer: Well, she asked about his 'tension again, and it get stupider and stupider . . . Then he say he want you.

Beverly: And that was stupid, too, aye?

Jennifer: Yeah . . . Stupidest of all was when she say "Heat o' the lions is not enough."

Beverly: "Heat of the . . . " [*Quickly*] Okay, go on.

Jennifer: She say she say her say.

Beverly: What?

Jennifer [*Slowly*]: She . . . say . . . she . . . say . . . her . . . say!

Beverly: What did *he* say?

Jennifer: He say he understand and will think about it.

Beverly: You sure?

Jennifer: Sure I'm sure. After that it sound like he was goin', and I didn't want Mama find me listenin, so I gone to the kitchen.

Beverly *hugs* **Jennifer.**

Beverly: Thanks, Jen-Jen. You set my mind at ease, somewhat.
Jennifer: You and Lionel gettin married?
Beverly: Don't you think it's time? I wish I knew what he was thinking, though. Anyway, she was on my side. Yet I can't figure out . . . Considering how much Aunty talks against Lionel . . . how she could bring herself to encourage him to marry me.
Jennifer: I know why. So that when you married she could dance to your weddin!

Jennifer *bursts into laughter at her joke.* **Beverly** *smiles. Lights quickly fade.*

ACT TWO

Scene 1. Early evening, the same day, in Merline's front room

Beverly *sits in the armchair basting the hem of one of* **Jennifer**'*s skirts.* **Merline** *enters wearing one of her good cotton shifts, stockings, and pumps. Her hair is in curlers and she carries a comb, which she passes to* **Beverly.**

Merline: Here. You know how to fix these things, and don' take long. Matilda down the road waitin. I joinin her in The Beautiful Daughters of the Empire.

Beverly *begins taking out the curlers and the curls.*

Beverly: She doesn't have to pass any test, aye? Not with those legs look like cane-stalks.
Merline: Looks ain't everything. If you know what good for you, you would join, too.
Beverly: I don't believe in lodges.

Merline *twirls around.*

Merline: My slip hangin?
Beverly: If it was I would tell you.
Merline: How I look?
Beverly: All right.
Merline: Don' wan' no craziness from you and Jennifer when I gone.

Beverly: Tell Jennifer that; she's the child.
Merline [*Shouting*]: Hey you, Jennifer!
Jennifer [*Within*]: Yes, ma'am!
Merline: When you finish eatin, wash dem dishes then make sure the buckets full. I don' want no sperrits beatin me tonight. [*To* **Beverly**] Keep her inside this house. I don' want her strayin 'bout like potcake* dog. You hear me? . . . Lord, way I put that lodge card? . . . You hear me? [*Goes out and returns carrying a sweater, an inappropriate-looking hat and a miniscule handbag, into which she stuffs a lodge book.* **Beverly** *regards the hat with distaste.*] Remember no ring play for Jennifer. [*Puts on sweater and hat.*] That make her woman before time.
Beverly: You have to put on that ugly hat?
Merline: On principle; draft fallin'.
Beverly: It looks silly.
Merline: Let it look silly, once it protect my mole. Remember, keep Jennifer in this house, and if Mr. Joseph come round drive him to do what right, not just visit-visit when my back turn. Next thing you know: baby!
Beverly: That all you can think of?
Merline: I gatta think for you, your ma, and them neighbours. None of we is a law unto weself. [*Heads for the front exit.*] Don' do nothin you wouldn' wan' hear 'bout tomorrow.

Merline *leaves.* **Jennifer** *enters from behind the curtains, goes to* **Beverly** *and holds up the skirt for inspection.*

Jennifer: You finish this, Bev?
Beverly: Soon done.

*Bahamian dialect for "mongrel."

Jennifer: You want me to put on my bathing water now?
Beverly: Tell you what. [*Takes coins from a coin purse on the table.*] I want to read up on some jobs. Go to the Chinese for the *Tribune* for me, please.
Jennifer: Not the drugstore? Is nearer.
Beverly: The Chinese cheaper. And if Lionel here when you come back, what you supposed to say?
Jennifer: Good evenin.
Beverly: Right! Then you could go play till I call you.

Jennifer *runs out.* **Beverly** *picks up the skirt, with her back turned to the front entrance.* **Lionel** *enters, with a package behind his back, and soft-shoes behind her. He places one hand over her eyes.*

Lionel: Turn round slowly, eyes closed . . . Guess who?

He takes away his hand. She faces him, eyes closed. He kisses her lips and steers her to the sofa.

Beverly: Tastes like Lionel.
Lionel [*Laughing*]: In here is like a church. Where's the public?
Beverly: One went to Lodge and the other to the Chinese for *Tribune.*
Lionel: But the Chinese don't sell *Tribune.*
Beverly: They're a longer way off, though. [**Lionel** *laughs.*] I was hoping you'd come and we would be alone—for once. Then Lodge doesn't come out till late. [*Kisses* **Lionel.**]
Lionel: Witch. So that's why you held back today . . . Wait; I bought something for you. You'll like it a lot, and it'll show I'm always thinking of you.
Beverly: Flowers?
Lionel: Nope.

Beverly: A wearing something?
Lionel: Wrong again.
Beverly: Not jewellery? Well, if it isn't a wearing something, I can't guess.

Lionel *gives* **Beverly** *the package. She opens it to find a box of chocolates and holds the box one moment in silence.*

Lionel: Sweets for the sweet. [*Silence.*] You don't seem glad . . . What's the matter, Bev? Don't tell me you're still mad from today.
Beverly: You said you wanted me. To Auntie.
Lionel: I did . . . I do.
Beverly: Then you bring me chocolates, that's all. Auntie thinks you're using me.
Lionel: She is wrong.
Beverly: I told her so this morning.
Lionel: You stuck up for me? [*Kisses her.*] She as much as ordered me to marry you or bring back your money . . . We'll get married.
Beverly: When?
Lionel: Maybe I'm marrying you because I can't come up with your eight hundred dollars.
Beverly: When?
Lionel: Whenever you say.
Beverly: What about your night classes?
Lionel: I'll cancel them.
Beverly: Seriously? Why?
Lionel: How you mean why? *One*—we're engaged. *Two*—you reminded me. *Three*—your aunt preached a very good sermon. *Four*—you stood up for me. *Five*—I'll probably have to get married someday, so it might as well be to you. [*Ducks a playful blow she sends his way.*] *Six*—I'm used to you, and *seven*—I think I need you.

Beverly: And you love me?
Lionel: Passionately.
Beverly: So how about a week from Sunday?
Lionel: That's pretty short notice. We'll need more than a week to take blood tests, publish banns, and buy the licence. I'll check the details on Monday.

Jennifer *is heard singing offstage.* **Beverly** *and* **Lionel** *separate.*

Jennifer:

Brown girl in the ring,
Tra la la la la.
Brown girl in the ring,
Tra la la la la.
Brown girl in the ring,
Tra la la la la.
And she looks like the sugar in the plum
Plum-plum!

Jennifer *enters and gives the newspaper to* **Beverly.**

Jennifer: Good evenin, Lionel.
Lionel: Hiya, princess. So we meet again.
Jennifer: You make mistake, Bev. The Chinese don' sell *Tribune,* so I had to turn back and get it at the drugstore like I wanted to in the first place. See your change.
Beverly: You can keep it.
Jennifer: They playin ring-play. I could go? [**Beverly** *pretends to hesitate.*] Hey, Bev? I won' stay long.
Beverly: Okay, go, but make sure come when I call you.

Jennifer *bounces off.* **Beverly** *sits in the armchair and scans the ads while* **Lionel** *stands behind her, caressing her neck.*

Beverly: Now, if there's a job here that suits me I'll be on the way. Just what we need to start us off. . . . Ah, here's one.

Lionel: Leave the business, Bev. Time for that later.

Beverly [*Reading.*]: "Wanted: efficient secretary, Davies Construction Company."

Lionel *freezes in position.*

Beverly: Why you so still all of a sudden?

Lionel: A roach just crawled over my grave.

Beverly: Cut out the spooky talk. If I got this job we'd both be working in construction.

Lionel *snatches the newspaper away, tosses it onto the table and pulls* **Beverly** *to her feet.*

Lionel: Let that wait for Monday. Tonight is ours. Let's play-play. I'll play the daddy, and you'll play the mommy.

Beverly: And the house is quiet. Think they'll stay away for once?

Lionel: You know those lodge meetings.

Beverly: And Jen-Jen really likes ring-play.

Beverly *and* **Lionel** *kiss and go out through the curtains at back.* **Children** *burst onstage and assemble in formation to play jump-in dance.*

Children:

Brown girl in the ring,
Tra la la la la.
Brown girl in the ring,
Tra la la la la.

Brown girl in the ring,
Tra la la la la.
And she looks like the sugar in the plum
Plum-plum!

Go look for your lover,
Tra la la la la.
Go look for your lover,
Tra la la la la.
Go look for your lover,
Tra la la la la.
And she looks like the sugar in the plum
Plum-plum!

Lights fade.

ACT TWO

Scene 2. The same evening in the Davies living-room

Erma *sits in an armchair with the table lamp off.* **Harold** *appears in the doorway and peers into the room.*

Harold: Erma, you here?
Erma: I here.

Harold *enters and turns on the light.*

Harold: Why not turn on the light? The bill's paid up.
Erma: I thinking.
Harold: Light never stopped anyone from thinking . . . You want to see me? You'll have to make it quick. My flight leaves in two hours.
Erma: You won' be going on that flight.
Harold: I thought we went over that before. I made it patently clear that this is a business trip and I am going alone.
Erma: Don' talk high and mighty to me, Harold. Isn't me causin you to cancel your trip.
Harold: Who else but you would look for an excuse to keep me in this pen?
Erma: Ask Sonia.
Harold: Why? What's going on here? You threw a tantrum this morning because I had a few drinks last night. All that weepy, soppy stuff about staying home and talking to you. Now I'm talking to you, you won't even spare me an explanation. What's this about

Sonia? I noticed neither of you ate supper. One of your silent battles?

Erma: I ain' fighting no battle. [*Stands.*] Sonia pregnant, Harold.

Harold *stands still, rooted by shock.*

Harold: I must be hearing things. Say that again.

Erma: Sonia *pregnant*. I make her tell me while you been eatin. [*Silence.*] She pregnant. I know from this mornin.

Harold: And didn't say anything? What kind of mother are you?

Erma: I was too sick to say anything.

Harold: Pregnant. Can't be. [*Going to the door and shouting*] Sonia! Sonia, I want to see you right now! [*Crosses to the bar and pours a drink.*]

Erma: That won' help.

Sonia *comes in cautiously, as if expecting a blow.* **Harold** *turns on her.*

Harold: Tell me it isn't true, Sonia. I can take a joke as well as the next man. [*Silence.*] By damn, it is true! [*Faces* **Erma.**] You call yourself a mother and don't know what's going on under your own roof?

Erma: Yeah, blame me. You didn't have no part in bringing her into this world.

Harold: Raising girls and telling them things they should know is woman's work, but you were too busy spying on me to keep track of what was happening right under your nose.

Sonia: No use accusing Mother. She didn't know. Nobody knew but me and him.

Harold: Who is this "him"? . . . Talk, or so help me I'll beat it outa you!
Erma: Touch her, you gat to touch me, too!
Harold [*Ignoring* **Erma**]: Who was he? The fellow you were singing along with in the office today?
Erma: Singing?
Sonia: Leave Lionel out of this.

Harold *moves threateningly towards* **Sonia.**

Harold: Who was the son-of-a-bitch? Tell me so I can get my gun and blast his ass!
Erma: Control yourself, Harold. Look at me; I gat as much reason to be upset, but I calm.
Harold: You aiding and abetting her in her stubbornness . . . Look; I devoted my life to building a sound business reputation. Now, thanks to this nitwit, my name will be mud in business circles. [*To* **Sonia**] For the last time—*who*?
Sonia: A minister.
Harold: You went with a clergyman?
Sonia: Not a clergyman. A government minister.
Harold: Holy Moses! . . . Minister or no minister, he'll do right by you.
Erma [*To* **Sonia**]: Tell him the rest.
Sonia: He's married.
Harold: What? Why you want to mix with a married man?
Erma: The sins of the father being visited on the children.
Harold [*To* **Erma**]: Cut that shit! [*To* **Sonia**] If you said you played around with a boy from school and something like this happened, I'd still be mad as hell, but at least I might look on it as a childish mistake. Going around with a married man is not a childish mistake. Sonia—why?
Sonia: He made me feel important.

Harold: So importance comes in and good breeding goes out! After all our planning, this is the thanks we get.
Sonia: I didn't do it on purpose.
Erma: Don' lie. You do it from rebellion. It was your way of gettin back at us for turnin you into a bookworm . . . You don' understand, Sonia. I wanted you to skip my mistake, but trying to save you, I fail. I drive you to it through being too hard.

Harold *pours another drink and stands with his back to the women.* **Sonia** *stands still.* **Erma** *sits in her armchair.*

Erma: That dream last night. Was a warnin.
Harold: Time for dreaming past, Erma.
Erma: No, Harold. I learn from dreams. I didn' understand the meaning of this one till now. Was a warnin, a warnin against punishing my child for my own mistake. A warnin against tryin to make her into what I never was.

Harold *and* **Sonia** *remain standing, frozen, while* **Erma** *tells her dream.*

Erma: I dream like I was in this building when I hear a girl-child scream from outside that a red man after her to kill her. I run out, thinking somehow I could fight off the danger, hoping someone—my lover—would help her, too. You know how mix up dreams are . . . We run in and out the building—upstairs and downstairs, the girl screamin all the time, "Help! He after me to kill me." [*Pause.*] Soon a crowd was followin' us. Police come and stand on the stairs jus' ahead. The girl run up to them: "Help! He comin' this way!" Then she rushed downstairs. I was about to haul after her when one mind tell me look up. I look up and there was this man . . . He walk straight pass the police like they wasn' there. And the stranges thing was, they keep lookin in the direction they expect him to come from. When I see that, I take to my heels. I catch up with the child, and we dashed past offices on the bottom floor. I was ahead. In front of us was a sort of basement full of pipes. I dart in there. The lights was on. There was scarcely any hiding-place. I squeeze 'gainst a wall, between a door and a window with the little girl scrunched up next to me . . . We could hear the man breathing heavy as he draw near. Suddenly the girl run from 'side me and start looking for the switch to turn the light off. I was never so scared. I motion to her not to try—he would see her—but it was too late. While she was standing there confused, the door swing open. The man didn' come in, but I could see the top half of his body. He wasn' red like she said. He was fat and old. He stand there, looking at the child trap under the light. Any moment I thought to hear a gunshot, but no! The man just break into the bitterest row 'gainst love and alcohol . . . Seem like he hunt down the child to stop her being like his daughter. His daughter did love a man he was against and she married him. When I hear that I feel so relieved.

Sonia: Why didn't the police see him?

Erma: Maybe he wasn' a flesh-and-bone man. He didn' kill the child like she said he would.

Sonia: Maybe he did. Maybe it wasn't a flesh-and-bone killing.

Harold *faces them abruptly.*

Harold: Enough nonsense. Now is time for action. [*To*

Sonia] This minister of yours—does he know of your condition?

Sonia: Of course he does! And he is not *my* minister. He gave me money for an abortion. Mother has it.

Harold: Abortion. You plan on having one?

Erma: You should know better than that.

Sonia: Daddy, you try and force me to and I'll leave home!

Harold: I was not suggesting an abortion; I just wondered what your attitude to it was. Glad to see you're not altogether hopeless . . . You'll have to get married.

Sonia: Why?

Harold: To protect yourself against other men with itchy trousers who might make you feel "important." No daughter of mine gonna keep getting the runaround.

Erma: Girl, you might as well change your clothes. Night classes finish. We know the horse out of the stable, but the least we can do is shut the door so the whole island won't see the stable empty.

Sonia *does not move.*

Erma: Well?

Sonia: I got to go to class tonight. To meet somebody.

Silence. **Harold** *rests his head on his hands.*

Erma: Who?

Sonia: Lionel.

Harold *looks interested.*

Erma: Lionel?

Harold: Lionel Joseph. One of our masons. She was singing with him in the office this morning.

Erma: What you take yourself for—a public slop bucket? Nothin' more than a bowl for every Tom, Dick, and Harry to empty his bladder into? Hey? [*Shakes* **Sonia.**] Answer me, slut! Answer me! [**Erma** *coughs and gasps for breath.* **Harold** *rushes to her side.*]

Harold: Quiet yourself. [*To* **Sonia**] Go bring a glass of water and a tranquillizer. Hurry!

Sonia *goes out.* **Harold** *pats* **Erma's** *face.* **Sonia** *returns with a glass containing a fizzy mixture.* **Harold** *gives the drink to* **Erma** *and holds her in his arms until she shows signs of reviving.*

Harold: Don't worry; I'll handle things. Don't worry. [*Still holding* **Erma,** *to* **Sonia**] If you don't want it on your conscience that you killed your own mother, do as I say. Go to class and meet Joseph like you planned, but make sure bring him back with you.

Sonia: Why?

Harold: Don't stand there askin questions. Move! [**Sonia** *looks at* **Erma**.] Get out of here. She'll be all right—for now.

Sonia *goes out, after flashing another glance at* **Erma**.

Erma: I hear you. What you think you doin', sendin her to meet that man?

Harold: I'm looking after our interests. Furthermore, if she wanted to meet Joseph she would, no matter what we said. Look . . . She'll keep the baby, but on my terms. She must get married.

Erma: To who? Joseph?

Harold: She could do worse.

Erma: What if he won' have her?

Harold: He will. I have yet to meet a man who can't be bought for a price . . . He might kick at the idea for a start, but if he's half as ambitious as I think he is, he'll lean my way eventually.

Erma: Love don' count in all this?

Harold: You and your love. Sometimes love can be an inconvenience. This is one of those times . . . It's dog eat dog, Erma.

Silence. Blackout.

ACT TWO

Scene 3. 10:00 P.M. that night in Merline's front room

Beverly *is finishing off* **Jennifer's** *skirt. On the table lies the box of chocolates, open. The* **Tribune**, *with the Davies advertisement cut out, covers the floor.* **Merline** *enters downstage, humming "Jesus Paid It All." She walks briskly, obviously pleased with her outing. She enters by the front steps.*

Merline: You still on that one skirt?

Beverly: I put it away for a while . . . How was Lodge?

Merline: If you wan' know you shoulda come. [*Takes off her shoes.*] Lordie, these corn killin' me . . . We make arrangement for the yearly procession. [*Folds her sweater.*]

Beverly: Matilda Bascombe run her mouth as usual?

Merline: Not overmuch. She only does talk to be sociable anyway.

Beverly: Whose reputation she tear apart in order to be sociable?

Merline: She ain' tear no reputation. She just mention somethin' concernin' the people she work for . . . Seem like the oldest gal wit' child.

Beverly: I knew it! Spreading scandal.

Merline: 'Tain' no scandal; is warnin. Take care, 'cause Trouble don' pick and choose who to come to. Das why I always behind you not to let dese worthless man mess with you just so . . . Jennifer do like I say? [*Does not wait for an answer but goes out with sweater, hat, and shoes. Can be heard after a few seconds*] No, no, can' be! [*Erupts into the front room and confronts* **Beverly**.] You, miss lady, ent I leave you in charge?

Beverly: What's the matter?

Merline: Slackness, das the matter! When I left, the last word out my mouth was for Jennifer to go to the faucet, den make ready for bed. Now I come back to find the water buckets empty as Kaiyer back pocket and no Jennifer in sight.

Beverly: She just went for water to bathe.

Merline: What she was doin' before?

Beverly: Washing dishes.

Merline [*Regarding* **Beverly** *with scorn*]: Come again . . . If you had to lie for shelter you would sleep outdoors.

Beverly *bites into a chocolate.*

Merline: Ay, ay! Candy and all. Who own dem?

Beverly: As you can see—me. Lionel brought them.

Merline: What for?

Beverly: How you mean what for?

Merline: Man don' buy candy just to spend money . . . Somethin' gotta give.

Beverly: There you go again.

Merline: Judas sell Christ for thirty pieces of silver. [*Holds up the chocolate box.*] Dis all Lion-el think you worth?

Beverly: Leave him alone! [*Snaps the thread on the skirt as if it were* **Merline's** *neck, snatches up the box, and leaves the room.*]

Merline *picks up the newspaper and leafs through it. She glances with interest at the space where the ad was, folds the newspaper, and lays it on the table. She turns to go as* **Beverly** *returns with a skirt of her own and resumes her seat.* **Merline** *goes out through the curtains; in the background her voice can* *be heard reprimanding the now-bathing* **Jennifer. Beverly** *grimaces at the noise.*

Merline: Now wash your back or in you go again! I never yet see a child get so dirty just by bein' in the house. [*Re-enters grumbling, wearing a duster and carrying a comb and plastic container filled with hair-curlers. These she gives to* **Beverly**.] Here. Set my hair agen.

Looking pained, **Beverly** *puts aside the skirt and drags her chair to the table.* **Merline** *sits in the chair while* **Beverly** *sits on the dining-table.*

Merline: You never hear dat woman who sit on table never get married?

Beverly: That's old people's superstition. Furthermore, Lionel and I *are* getting married.

Merline [*Jerking her head upright*]: When?

Beverly: A week from Sunday, I hope.

Merline: In church?

Beverly: Where else?

Merline: Ain' gon be no week from Sunday, then. You have to publish banns at least three weeks before the wedding. Lion-el ain' tell you?

Beverly: He said something about banns, but I wasn't listening . . . Anyway, we could use the extra time to plan.

Merline: Well, well, well! Just goes to show—you only past everything when you dead . . . But I could swear that young man was up to no good. You should see he face when I order him to choose you or bring back your money.

Beverly: Auntie Merl, you had no business interfering. Still, Lionel called your bluff.

Merline: 'Cause he didn' have the money?

Beverly: What you hinting at?

Merline: No need to hint. When I talked to him today he wasn' in no mind for weddin. Hedge and hedge to duck makin' a straight answer. All about he didn' wan' rush but he still wan' you. Right then I know he had one thing in mind: jump in bed wit' you first chance he get.

Beverly *shakes her head in disbelief.*

Merline: Then he come round like Satan in Easter Sunday suit, bringin candy. [*Laughs.*] Some deal in sweet talk. He deal in sweet taste. [*Laughs again.*]

Beverly: Auntie Merl, you always ready to twist the simplest thing into wickedness!

Merline: Nobody could tell me he didn' know weddin take more than one week to arrange.

Beverly: *I* thought that, not him!

Silence.

Merline: Three weeks . . . That will give him time to back down.

Beverly: No!

Merline [*Turning to stare at* **Beverly**]: Unless he ain' get what he did come for.

Silence. The women watch each other. **Beverly** *wrenches her eyes from* **Merline***'s steady gaze and runs from the room.* **Merline** *thinks for a second, then sighs deeply, wearily.*

Merline: So das the way it was. Mercy, mercy me.

Blackout.

ACT TWO

Scene 4. About 11:00 P.M. the same night in the Davies living-room

Harold Davies *sits reading the evening paper while from the back comes the sound of a television set turned up loud.* **Harold** *registers annoyance, goes to the upstage exit, and shouts through.*

Harold: Turn that noise down! There are other people in this house besides you all!

The sound diminishes. **Harold** *returns to his chair.* **Erma** *enters with her crocheting and sits in her special chair.*

Harold: Why they have to make such a racket? Shouldn't they be in bed?

Erma: They sense something going on. I tell them watch T.V. That way they won' be underfoot when Sonia comes . . . Harold, the more I think 'bout it, the less I like what you plannin to do. Buyin a husband for Sonia.

Harold: I am not buying anything for anyone. She likes the young man, and he might like her, too, for all we know. I didn't bring them together, but I sure as hell won't be the one to keep them apart.

Erma: Let her have the baby without gettin married.

Harold: Not on your life!

Erma: I don' see why not. Look, when people hear Sonia pregnant I is the one they'll laugh at. Her disgrace is mine . . . Don' think I like the idea of scandal; I don't. I work all my life for you and these children to be respectable, to walk with your heads high. Now I have to hang my head. Lord knows I rather do that and make Sonia face up to one mistake than compel her to make another one.

Harold: No one is compelling, so stop talking bullshit!

Erma: You always call the truth bullshit . . . I make the mistake of givin my best years to a man who only use me for doormat to wipe his foot after he dirty it in other woman muck . . . I didn' wan' Sonia to suck sorrows before she had chance to live.

Harold: Suck sorrows! Let her wreck my image and you won't have to exaggerate.

Erma: Your image, Harold? Your image is nothin but a skeleton.

Harold: Skeleton or not, I'll do my damnedest to preserve it. [*Ominously*] No matter what you say.

Erma: What if I won' stand by and watch you ruin her life?

Harold: You could do the next best thing. This island is not *that* small.

Erma: You mean it! You really mean it. You would be happy if I left so you could bring your floozies into my house . . . Not a thing like it! I staying right here. She gon' need me when your plans break her. [*Rises.*] But I refuse to be in this room when you set your trap.

Erma *leaves with her crocheting.* **Harold** *takes up his newspaper. There is silence, then the sound of the T.V., then footsteps.* **Sonia** *looks in.*

Sonia: Lionel is here, Daddy.

Harold: Bring him in.

Sonia *vanishes.* **Harold** *casts his features into a fatherly mould as he greets* **Lionel.** *At first* **Lionel** *is wary of the older man, but he warms gradually to* **Harold's** *attentiveness, although he cannot quite account for it.* **Sonia** *hovers in the background, uncertain whether to go or stay.*

Harold: Well, Joseph, you sure moved fast with Sonia. I knew there must have been something behind that sing-along you conducted at the office this morning. Make friends with the daughter to get next to the father, hey?

Lionel: I did not make friends with Sonia to get next to you, sir.

Harold: Never mind, never mind; I understand. We men are only human, after all. What you having?

Lionel: Nothing, sir.

Harold: Come, come. It's not every day that we meet for a chat, you know. Which reminds me. I saw Miller this afternoon. I see why you two can't get on. He thinks you're a joke. A greenhorn without a future.

Lionel: Wishful thinking on his part, sir. Right now I have more skill in my little finger than he's got in his whole body.

Harold: Right; stand by your guns . . . I didn't pay him much mind, though. I thought in time you'd prove that you are no joke, but a force to reckon with.

Lionel: Thank you, sir.

Harold: I've got faith in you, Joseph. In your ability.

Lionel: I'm glad to hear that, sir.

Harold: My drink is Scotch. What's yours?

Lionel *considers.*

Harold: Don't make me drink alone.

Lionel: Beer'll be fine.
Harold [*To* **Sonia**]: Get a beer for Mr. Joseph.

Sonia *goes out.* **Harold** *sips his drink.*

Lionel: How did you start in business, sir?
Harold: As a plumbing contractor. Then I went into selling general building supplies. From there was a short step to hiring painters, carpenters, masons—men with experience. In those days I was the foreman—here, there, all over the place. That is changed, of course . . . But I still keep close watch over everything . . . From selling supplies we branched into construction of low-income homes, duplex apartments, one-storey structures. We barely kept our head above water. In the construction industry the thing is, though, to get into the home-building sector so that when things slow down in banking and hotel construction you have something to fall back on.
Lionel: I see.
Harold: Don't get me wrong. That's not to say I wouldn't dirty my hands if something really big came along.
Lionel: Like what? A hospital?

They laugh.

Harold: No. That's batting out of my league—at least for the present . . . I was thinking more of something I could cut my teeth on without bruising my mouth. Like a school, for instance. A medium-sized high school on one of the larger islands. Now if I got such a contract I'd really be going to town.

Sonia *enters with a glass of beer and a beer can on a tray.*

She gives the beer to **Lionel**, *places the tray on the table beside him, and sits in an inconspicuous position.*

Harold [*Continuing to fantasize*]: Yes, sirree, I would really have it made. That would be all I need to turn from an "up-and-coming" businessman into a big shot. Just one good government contract.

Lionel: You might get it one day.

Harold: Yeah. When chicken get teeth. [*Pauses. Sips. The glimmering of an idea comes to him. He brightens visibly.*] Come to think of it, might not be so far-fetched after all. Only calls for li'l connections: pulling a string here, dropping the right name there, a whispered word in someone's ear. [*Pauses. Thinks.*]

Lionel *sips his beer. There is silence for the count of five.*

Sonia: Daddy, let Lionel tell you his philosophy.

Harold *drops out of his reverie and looks from* **Sonia** *and* **Lionel** *and at* **Sonia** *again.*

Harold: What?

Sonia: You looked a hundred miles away . . . Let Lionel tell you his philosophy.

Harold *looks expectantly at* **Lionel** *and listens with half his attention. The other half is centred on a blossoming idea. He gives the impression of being excited in a controlled fashion. This* **Lionel** *mistakes for interest; he is not altogether wrong.*

Lionel: Doesn't take much telling. [*Pauses, then continues in a rush*] Boils down to this: to get somewhere, a man must know where he wants to go, what it takes to get there, how to go about getting what it takes—and he must believe he can make it. Too often people get side-tracked by the "you-can'ters," the prophets of doom . . . I listened myself, for a time, and I almost believed them, but a small voice inside me rejected their way of thinking. How come they knew so much? They tried everything? That was when I figured that maybe the "you-can'ters" weren't God after all. They might just be people who failed for a number of reasons. Perhaps their goal wasn't cut out for them; perhaps they went about getting it the wrong way. Maybe they didn't stick with it long enough, or they doubted themselves, and they want me to doubt myself. I refuse to do that.

Silence.

Harold: Uh-huh. You could be a big-time crook if you wanted to be.

They all laugh.

Lionel: What's the challenge in flirting with the police? My goals are already set.

Harold *looks interested.*

Sonia: He wants to be a building contractor, too.
Harold: Well, let's hear your plans, Joseph.
Lionel: You see, we own this piece of property, me and my old lady.
Harold: Your mother.
Lionel: No. My fiancée.
Harold: You're practically married?
Lionel: Practically.

Lionel *sips his beer.* **Harold** *offers him a cigarette and lights it while* **Sonia** *watches. In the background is the sound of the television turned up loud and little girls' laughter.*

Harold [*To* **Sonia**]: Go quiet them. Sing them a lullaby or something.

Sonia *goes out.*

Harold: Time for children, women, and old people to be in bed. [*Laughs.*] We don't qualify.

The television is turned off. There are grumbles from within, then silence for the count of three.

Lionel: Like I was saying, we own this piece of property. We'll build a house—duplex-style—rent part, and live in part. From there the sky's the limit. Ten to fifteen years should see me on my feet.

Harold: Makes good sense. Erma and me started out that way. Both of us worked; then we built this house and she stayed home to run it . . . Since then we don't seem to see eye to eye, somehow. We don't seem to want the same things—at least not in the same order. Centre of her world is this house and the children. Maybe I fit in somewhere. My world is larger. It keeps on growing. New situations. New faces . . . I suppose she feels cheated somehow. Understand? [**Lionel** *nods.*] She's got this notion that you can press a button and turn back time. Wants to be courted again, but I've lost interest. Would you believe I've outgrown my own wife?

Lionel: You wouldn't argue against marrying young, though. I'm twenty-five and Bev's just nineteen.

Harold: No. Marrying young is okay once it's to the right person and you don't allow things to get stale. Do things together. Laugh with each other.

Lionel: Laugh?

Harold: Yeah . . . Erma was always too serious; she never broke out of it. A man needs a woman who is fun to be with *some* of the time. Imagine coming home after a hard day only to hear how this one sprained a fingernail or that one broke a straw . . . Travel; join clubs. You know? Of course your girl should still be able to boil water without burning it. [*Smiles.*] No, my main regret is not having any sons, only five girls.

Lionel: What's wrong with girls?

Harold: Everything.

Lionel *looks puzzled.*

Harold: Look. Girls don't guarantee a man's name. I'm Davies. The moment one of them gets married, she drops my name. Good for her, but where does it leave me? . . . Besides that, there ain't much you can do with girls in the way of entertainment. I mean, I'm no good at sewing doll clothes . . . Now if one of them was a boy at least on weekends I'd have someone to go fishing with . . . But listen. Listen to this. This is the biggy. [*He is beginning to feel his drinks.*] *Girls are a casualty risk.* Poor lambs at the mercy of every two-legged wolf with an appetite. When I think of that I could cry . . . Me . . . a big man . . . crying. [*Laughs instead.*]

Lionel: I'm sure you need not worry, sir.

Harold: Call me Harold.

Lionel: Yes, sir . . . Harold.

Harold: Good. Yeah, I could cry. It isn't like I haven't worked hard for all I own: the business, the liquor store, this house, the apartments I rent. Property all over this island. I worked damned hard. Wouldn't you say so?

Lionel: Yes, Harold.

Harold: I'm telling you these things because we're friends and I know what I say here won't go beyond these walls. Got that?

Lionel: Yes, Harold.

Harold: Good . . . I'm not old, but I like to think ahead.

Lionel: Nothing wrong with that.

Harold: Wait a minute . . . Like I said, I like to think ahead, so I planned to make my will. You know? Here I am all ready to will my business to my first grandson, and guess what? [*Lowers his voice conspiratorially.*] The damned child promises to be a bastard!

To cover his shock **Lionel** *concentrates on his cigarette.*

Harold: Yeah. A bastard.

Lionel: Hard to believe.

Harold: True, though. Some hot-rod politician knocked Sonia up.

Lionel *looks up, surprised.*

Harold: Yeah. All those loyal party supporters out there [*Gesturing downstage*] and he picks on a sixteen-year-old girl. He flattered her awhile, but she grew up in a hurry when he gave her money for an abortion. Double-O-seven, licensed to kill. She refused, of course, and that's that . . . What to do? I never yet felt so helpless. [*Sadly*] We had such hopes for her. She would go off to school and come back to work in the office. And her first-born son—the son I never had—would inherit the business. High hopes exploded just so! [*Makes a puffing, plosive sound. Silence. Looks at* **Lionel**.] To tell the truth, when you walked in tonight that dead hope showed a sign of life. [*Pauses.*] Of course it doesn't make sense even dreaming that one man could be so big-hearted as to carry another man's burden. [*Pauses.*] I mean . . . it would take a man of vision, a dreamer of dreams, one who could look beyond the present to a glorious future as husband to Sonia and my partner in the business. That would take a man ready to risk growing.

Lionel *sits very still.*

Harold: When I saw you walk in tonight, I thought, *Here is the man, the father of my first grandson, the stone which the builders set at naught, that would become head of the corner* . . . "DAVIES, JOSEPH, AND SON, CONSTRUCTION, LIMITED." That sign blazed across my mind in a flash.

There is silence for the count of five. **Lionel** *rises, touched, apologetic.*

Lionel: You're forgetting something. I'm promised to someone else.

Harold: Promises are made to be broken. Anyway, what's so binding about an engagement? Listen, if you want to get somewhere today you can't afford the luxury of sentiment . . . I understand. You don't want to make a hasty decision. That wouldn't say much for you as a man of your word. I value your hesitation. I respect you for it, but remember, in the long run lasting things are what count. Passions cool. Think of your name. Make something of it.

Lionel: Sorry. I have to go. [*Moves to the exit.*]

Harold: Think of my offer over the week-end, then drop by the office Monday and we'll talk.

Lionel: Thanks for the drink.

Harold: Plenty more where that came from.

Lionel *leaves.* **Harold** *sighs heavily, like a man who has just finished a long race. He stands a moment in thought, recalls his previous idea, goes to the upstage exit, listens to the silence, then goes out. In a moment he returns, preceded by* **Sonia**, *who wears a housecoat over her night-dress.* **Harold** *leads* **Sonia** *downstage.*

Harold [*Intensely and urgently*]: Why you didn't tell me Joseph was engaged?

Sonia: There wasn't time, and you chased me out, so . . .

Harold: You like him?

Sonia: A bit. He's interesting. You might get to meet Beverly, Lionel's fiancée, on Monday, if she doesn't change her mind.

Harold: Oh?

Sonia: He told me Beverly saw your ad and she might come for an interview.

Harold [*Half to himself*]: If she showed up on Monday and . . . [*Stops himself from revealing his thoughts. Shifts to another trend.*] You must have phone numbers for your ex-sweetheart. Direct numbers. Let me see them.

Sonia [*Looking uncomfortable*]: I'm not bothering with him anymore.

Harold: I am.

Sonia [*Tugging at* **Harold's** *arm*]: Daddy, what you planning to do? Don't call him. That's over and done with. Please don't rake up dead ashes.

Harold [*Shaking her off*]: Go get the number, if you don't want our family name broadcast by all the nosy secretaries.

Sonia *goes to the upstage door and turns.*

Sonia: He could ruin you.

She leaves. **Harold** *weaves to the liquor cabinet and pours another drink. He stands forestage with the glass in his hand.*

Harold: *Ruin* me? [*Laughs.*] Wouldn't say that. Why, he could be the *making* of me. [*Raises the glass in a toast.*] "DAVIES, JOSEPH AND SON, CONSTRUCTION."

Blackout.

ACT THREE

Scene 1. Eleven-thirty the following Monday morning in Harold Davies's outer office

The reception area is set up as in Act 1. **Beverly** *sits in an easy chair down left, looking elegant in the skirt she has hemmed, a matching blouse, and black shoes. Her black handbag rests on the floor beside the chair. The door to the inner office opens and* **Harold** *comes out, preceded by a* **young woman** *clutching a large envelope.*

Harold: Thanks for coming. Of course it's still too early to give a definite answer. After all, you're only the third for the morning, and as you can see [*with a wave of his hand in* **Beverly**'*s direction*], they just keep on coming.

Harold *walks the* **young woman** *to the exit down left.*

Harold: So in all fairness I really shouldn't decide 'til I interview several more applicants . . . If you're the lucky one—and your qualifications are so good, you might well be—I'll give you a call. 'Bye for now.

The **woman** *leaves.* **Harold** *approaches* **Beverly,** *who stands nervously fingering her manila envelope.*

Harold: Hello. I suppose you came about the job.
Beverly: Yes, sir.

She hands him the envelope. **Harold** *opens it and notices that she is still standing.*

Harold: Have a seat, Miss . . .
Beverly: Humes. Beverly Humes.

Beverly *sits.* **Harold** *lifts the top sheet from the envelope. It is a certificate bearing* **Beverly**'*s name.* **Harold** *turns his back and paces upstage and to the right, behind the desk. At a point below the filing cabinet he turns and surveys* **Beverly**.

Harold: Right you are, Beverly Angela Humes.

He flips cursorily through the other documents, replaces them, and half-sits on the front edge of the desk, facing **Beverly.**

Harold: Everything seems to be in order: birth certificate, health certificate, school record, professional diplomas, recommendations . . . Well, Miss Humes, you just landed yourself a job.
Beverly [*thunderstruck*]: How? You haven't asked me questions or anything.
Harold: Who says I must?
Beverly: I don't get it. That other girl—you told her you had to see more applicants.
Harold: And I did. I saw *you*.

He goes around the desk, pulls out a drawer, extracts a sign with black lettering on a white background, and shows it to **Beverly**. *It reads: "POSITION FILLED."*

Harold: This should take care of the rest. Be right with you.

Harold *exits left.* **Beverly**, *groping for an explanation for* **Harold**'*s sudden decision, takes out a compact from her bag and* *looks at her face critically. There is the sound of* **Harold** *returning.* **Beverly** *snaps her compact shut and puts it away as* **Harold** *reappears.*

Harold: That's that.

Beverly: Seems like a miracle.

Harold: Don't you believe it. Only miracles you come across these days are man-made.

Beverly: It happened so quick. Sir, you don't want to look closer at my papers?

Harold: Why? They forgeries? [**Beverly** *smiles nervously.*] Come, relax. When you've been around as long as me you develop a knack for judging quality just by looking. One look at you said you were quality. [*Holds her envelope.*] This comes in handy, but this [*Tapping his skull*] and this [*His eye*]—they're the judges. [*Passes the envelope to her.*]

Beverly: Don't you want details?

Harold: Since you insist. Let's have a summary of what's in your envelope.

Beverly [*In a rush*]: I was born and grew up on Eleuthera. I came to Nassau three years ago and spent two years at Technical and one year at Wellington Bank before they closed. I can take dictation, transcribe using a dictaphone, type up to eighty words a minute, do some book-keeping and filing, and operate most copy machines, including the Xerox office models, the A.B. Dick Electroflax, spirit duplicators, and the Gestetner ink roller. I've also made up reports and paysheets and spent two weeks at a switchboard . . . That's about all.

Harold: We can use you, believe me. The question is whether you'll agree to stay. See, I'm out most times, so you will have to be in charge. Not everyone can work long periods on their own.

Beverly: I don't mind being without company.

Harold: Good. You'll be in charge of messages and appointments, as well as being diplomatic with difficult workers and customers . . . How's your patience? In good condition?

Beverly: Oh, yes, sir. It'll hold up.

Harold: With that attitude, routine won't bore you. Correspondence, orders, and Customs entries will come like playing dollhouse. [*Thinks.*] One more thing—travel . . . I move around a lot. Going to Miami this evening as a matter of fact. When I have to travel you should see to arrangements: tickets, passport, reservations . . .

Beverly: Yes, sir.

Harold: On rare occasions I might ask you to come with me.

Beverly: In a business capacity.

Harold: But of course! [**Beverly** *looks relieved.*] I wouldn't ask you otherwise. Separate hotel rooms; strictly business. . . . Now, down to brass tacks. What did they pay you at the bank?

Beverly: A hundred dollars a week. To start with.

Harold: I'll make that one-fifty.

Beverly [*Relieved*]: Thank you, sir.

Harold: You'll find I always reward efficient service. Any questions?

Beverly: When may I start?

Harold: Now, if you like. [*Glances at his watch.*] Almost lunch-time. What say you spend a few minutes looking 'round the office, then after . . . [*The telephone on the desk rings.* **Harold** *answers it.*] Yes, speaking . . . The minister returning my call? Very good. One moment, please. [*To* **Beverly**] Transfer this to the other line, will you?

He goes into the inner office and shuts the door. **Beverly** *hangs up the receiver then walks around, becoming used to the office. She opens a few drawers in the desk, looks briefly into the filing cabinet, and returns to the desk. She sits on the swivel chair, testing its feel. It is too high. She wheels the chair down to the right of the desk and is about to adjust the height-control knob but straightens on hearing footsteps.* **Lionel** *enters down left.* **Beverly** *moves towards him, stops, and looks in the direction of the inner office.* **Lionel** *stands still when he sees her hesitation, unsure what* **Harold** *has told her.*

Beverly: Lionel, what are you doing here?
Lionel: I work for this company. Or at least I used to.

Beverly *latches onto* **Lionel**'*s first sentence.*

Beverly: You said your boss was named Miller.
Lionel: He's only the foreman. Where's Davies?
Beverly: In his office, on the phone talking to . . .
Lionel: Never mind all that. It doesn't give me much time.
Beverly: Time for what?
Lionel: Bev, I've got to talk to you.
Beverly: Where were you all week-end?
Lionel: In hell. Trying to figure something out. Then when I thought of the ad it all seemed to fit. I thought I should warn you.
Beverly: Warn me? Against what?
Lionel [*Pointing at the upstage door*]: Against *him.*
Beverly: Why? He's been so kind, giving me the job without any questions; he even upped my salary.
Lionel: *That's* what he's up to! Bev, can't you see, the whole thing is a trap set by him, his daughter, and wife.
Beverly: Trap? Daughter? Wife?
Lionel: Bev, you only got this job because you're connected with me.

Beverly: Now that's where you're wrong. I got this job because I'm 'specially qualified . . .

Lionel: So are a hundred other girls.

Beverly: . . . and I have what it takes to run this office.

Lionel: He's got you brainwashed. We're leaving here now, Bev! Now! [*Grabs her hand and moves towards the street-door.*]

Beverly [*Pulling away*]: You sick or something?

Lionel: Listen to me, Bev.

Beverly: I'm listening.

Lionel: And trust me.

Beverly: I've always trusted you.

Lionel: Then do like I say without questions. Where's your bag? [*Picks up* **Beverly**'*s handbag and grabs her arm.*] Let's get out of here!

Beverly: I can't just walk out without knowing why. It looks like a good chance, and we need the money, Lionel. I might not get an opportunity like this again.

Lionel: You will, and without falling into a trap. Now come on!

Beverly: What will he think?

Lionel: To hell with what he thinks; let's go.

Beverly: Not until you tell me what's so important I have to give up a good job because of it.

Lionel [*Restraining himself from lifting* **Beverly** *and taking her out of the room bodily*]: Okay, Bev, have it your way, but at least let's go outside. I'll explain it out there. I can't talk in here.

Beverly: Suppose he should come and find me gone?

Lionel: For Christ sake, maybe he'll think you went to the toilet!

Lionel *grabs* **Beverly**'*s arm again and steers her towards the exit. At that moment* **Harold** *steps out of his office.* **Lionel** *is prepared to proceed, but* **Beverly**, *embarrassed at being found* *in this position, strains to get away from him. He holds onto her while he confronts* **Harold**.

Harold: Would you mind saying where you're going with Miss Humes?

Lionel: She is my fiancée.

Harold: Really? You sure are busy, Joseph. Only last Friday you used this office like a playground with my daughter. Remember Sonia? She was your fiancée, too?

Lionel: What happened between me and Sonia was nothing more than accidental.

Harold: And the meeting Friday night after classes. That was accidental, too? Do better than that, Joseph.

Beverly, *enraged, turns on* **Lionel**.

Beverly: Last Friday night you were with me.

Harold: With you, too, aye? Must have gone to Sonia afterwards.

Beverly: Lionel, you . . . you had the heart to go to another woman after . . . How could you?

Lionel: Pay him no mind, Bev. Lies, that's all he's giving you. I didn't go to meet Sonia, but to cancel my classes like you said to. In fact, *she* seemed to be lying in wait for me. Don't believe him, Bev.

Beverly: Why not? It figures. You must have gotten that class idea from her . . . and when you saw me reading the ad you talked 'bout a roach being on your grave. You were afraid I would find out about her.

Lionel: You have it all wrong.

Beverly: Well, since you knew I needed a job and Mr. Davies needed a secretary why didn't you tell me so I could apply? Why you didn't say this was where you worked when I was reading the ad? You know why? Because you didn't want me to find out 'bout your two-timing; that's why.

Lionel [*Pointing to* **Harold**]: *He's* the reason I didn't want you here; he's the slimy roach, Bev. Won't you listen to me?

Beverly: Play them both; that was the plan? All weekend. All weekend I there waiting for you when you must have been seeing her . . . Now you try to make me give up the only job I've had in months. You must think I'm stupid. That what you think, Lionel? Is it?

Harold: Miss Humes, you may go to lunch now. Joseph and I have something to discuss.

Lionel: I don't have a fart to say to you, except you can go to hell and take your shittin job with you.

Beverly *moves towards the street exit.* **Lionel** *blocks her way.*

Lionel: Bev, it's not the way it seems. Stay, Bev, and hear what a rat you got mixed up with.

Harold: No need to downgrade yourself, Joseph. We all make mistakes.

Lionel *turns on* **Harold** *angrily.* **Beverly** *sees her opportunity and dashes from the room.* **Lionel** *approaches* **Harold** *menacingly.*

Lionel: Low-down rat is too good a name for you. Feeding me all that garbage 'bout poor little girls being victims of men's appetite. And all along you were setting me up to marry that whosoever-will piece of baggage you call daughter. Talk about offer. Here's my reply to your offer. [*Delivers a blow to* **Harold's** *midriff and stands over him.*] Fight. Get up and fight like a man . . .

Coward. I could piss on you, but you're not worth the water.

Harold *rises to a sitting position and feels his jaw where the blow landed.*

Harold: Go ahead; hit me again. I won't hit back. You know why? Because it wouldn't make sense, that's why. And because what I said to you Friday night was true. [*Rises to his feet.*] Hotheads like you think you know it all. You don't, not by a long shot. But I'll let you spill the poison out of your system . . . See. I'm up. Hit me again, Joseph. Go ahead. I won't fight back.

This approach confuses **Lionel**. **Harold** *notices the confusion and plays it for all it is worth.*

Harold: Look, I understand how you feel. Who wants someone else directing his life? I know I don't. We all like to feel we're in command. So you want success your way—the slow, hard way. I wouldn't try to stop you, not like muddleheads—Miller, for instance. Now to him you are nothing but a glorified water-boy. Why? Not just because you are bright and young, while he's a dull old fool, but because you've got gumption. More than he had at your age and in spite of greater obstacles. In spite of the circumstances of your birth. [**Lionel** *turns away in annoyance*] Don't say you're proud your pa was Haitian, that he lived in a chicken coop and had to scrape people grass for a living. Nothing wrong with scraping grass, it was honest work—at least *I* think so. But not everyone is like me. They hear your name and the only job they consider giving you is mending their pants or picking garbage from their yard. Work your ass off, wouldn't make much difference. They'll still bring their real work to Johnson or Smith, no matter if Johnson is drunk from sun-up to sun-down and Smith specialises in sloppy work and millionaire prices. No, you see, Johnson and Smith are "all-Bahamian," whatever that means. So? Might as well fight a brick wall—at least you could touch a brick wall. Can't touch hatred, prejudice, and class snobbery so easy. Maybe not at all . . . I should know—I came up from nothing—and there's no turning back . . . Look, Joseph, if I thought you were only a water-boy I wouldn't think of marrying you to my daughter . . . Why fight me? I'm your salvation. Come put your name next to mine on the sign: "Davies, Joseph and Son, Construction." [*Laughs*] Damn! Next thing you know, Haitian names will be the fashion. What you say?

Lionel *breaks out of his trance and musters up some of his old bravado, but not so convincingly.*

Lionel: Find yourself another sucker! [*He marches out, left.*]

Harold *stands a moment, looking at* **Beverly's** *chair. He wheels the chair into position behind the desk, looks at his watch, retreats to his private office and shuts the door. There is an empty set for the count of five. Then* **Erma** *enters, wearing a suit. She pauses and takes in the empty office and the closed upstage door.*

Erma [*Calling*]**:** Harold! [*Goes toward the door.*]

Harold *opens it and comes out. He does not seem pleased to see her.*

Harold: Oh, it's you.
Erma: That's all you can say to your one wife? You might ask how we managed at the doctor.
Harold: You'll tell me if you want to.
Erma: She's pregnant all right. Ten weeks.
Harold: What else is new? Where's Sonia now?
Erma: In the taxi outside.
Harold: Extravagant, aren't we?

This sarcasm is lost on **Erma**, *who looks around for traces of a new hireling.*

Erma: You get a new secret'ry?
Harold: Yes.
Erma: What she like? Pretty?
Harold [*Hedging*]: Passable. You told me about the doctor, Erma; now what else you want?
Erma: Sonia say you call that politician. I hope you ain' blackmailin him.
Harold: What a dirty little mind you have . . . I phoned to tell him what I thought about abortions. Now don't you think you should run along? We don't want to waste our grandson's future on a taxi, do we?
Erma: What 'bout the Joseph boy?
Harold: What about him? Listen. Whether anything happens or not between him and Sonia, she keeps the baby. Okay?
Erma: Miracle days ain' over yet! [*Moves to exit.*] You eatin home before your flight?
Harold: I'll catch a bite at the airport.
Erma: Take care.

Harold *kisses* **Erma** on the cheek as **Beverly** *enters.* **Beverly** *stops short in embarrassment, staring at the couple.* **Harold** *hurries to make introductions.*

Harold: Miss Humes, meet my wife. [*To* **Erma**] Miss Humes is the new secretary.
Beverly: Glad to meet you, Mrs. Davies.

Erma *stares at her.*

Erma: The feeling is mutual.

Sound of car horn outside, stage left. **Beverly** *rests her handbag on the desk and stands, undecided what to do next.* **Erma** *crosses to where she can take in* **Beverly's** *appearance.* **Harold** *looks slightly uncomfortable.*

Erma: More than just *passable,* I would say.

Beverly *glances from one to the other in puzzlement. There is the sound of footsteps as* **Sonia** *comes in.*

Sonia: Mother, hurry up! What's taking you so long? [*She enters, stops, and looks at the trio.*] Oh, excuse me.
Harold [*Rushing into the breach*]**:** Erma was on her way out.

Sonia *ignores him and crosses to* **Beverly.**

Sonia: I'm Sonia. You must be the new secretary.
Beverly: Yes. Beverly Humes.

Recognition dawns on **Sonia.**

Sonia: Then you must be Lionel's . . .

Erma *becomes more alert and ill at ease.* **Harold** *tries to ease the tension.*

Harold: Enough talk for now. Time to go.
Erma: Yes, let's go, Sonia. Chat with Miss Humes another time.

Erma *and* **Sonia** *move downstage.* **Beverly** *follows them, intrigued.*

Beverly [*To* **Sonia**]**:** What were you going to say?
Sonia: A friend of mine mentioned you.

The horn of the taxi blows insistently.

Beverly: What did he say?
Erma [*Grabbing* **Sonia***'s arm and leading her off*]**:** Later, Miss Humes. [*To* **Harold**] Have a safe trip.
Sonia: Bye, Daddy. So long, Miss Humes.

Erma *and* **Sonia** *go out.* **Beverly** *stands by the desk, mulling over what* **Sonia** *said—or didn't say.*

Beverly: Wonder what he told her about me, how they even got to meet.

Harold *crosses to her, all fatherly concern.*

Harold: Don't think about that now. [*Leads her to an easy chair, left.*] Have a seat. Relax. [*Stands over her.*] Joseph is a young man with an eye for the future. It shouldn't surprise you that he knows my daughter. If a girl wants to meet a man, no matter who he is, she'll find a way to meet him. And you can see for yourself how Sonia is: friendly as a child.
Beverly: True. But her knowing Lionel might be something good.

Harold: Who said it wasn't?

Beverly: The way you put it makes it . . . I thought . . . [*She stops, confused.*]

Harold: Thought what?

Beverly: Lionel warned me against you. Against all of you.

Harold: I guessed he would.

Beverly: He talked about a trap. Just now what Mrs. Davies said made me wonder if he was right.

Harold: I don't recall her saying anything.

Beverly: That I was more than "just passable." Why should she say that?

Harold *laughs, then hits on an explanation.*

Harold: She was giving her okay.

Beverly: Didn't sound that way.

Harold: Let me explain . . . While you were out I called home and praised you to the skies. Even told Erma I wanted you on this trip with me. Well, naturally, any careful wife would think twice about that, and Erma is more careful than most, so she came to inspect you. She obviously liked your good manners.

Beverly: What?

Harold: You see, Erma is not what you would call "educated." Consequently, people working here take her for a joke, so when someone like you comes along and says you're glad to meet her and sound like you mean it, why, she is flattered. Hence you're "more than just passable." Don't let her seeming coolness put you off; she's basically shy.

Beverly: Sir, you'd consider taking me on a trip when we scarcely know each other?

Harold: "Want to know someone? Work with him." That's my motto. In business we move fast; you should know that. Truth is, though, I desperately need someone from this side to sit in on meetings, take notes, witness signing of contracts, things like that.

Beverly: What you need is a lawyer.

Harold: Got one. He went on the morning flight. What I need most is a sensible secretary. My lawyer's shorthand is a bit rusty. [*Laughs at his joke.*]

Beverly: I see.

Harold: Face facts. It would be extra pay, and a change of scenery right now would do you good.

Beverly [*Thinking aloud*]: I'd have to go there anyway, to shop for the wedding.

Harold: Don't know about that!

Beverly [*Still to herself*]: Even without money to buy I still could window-shop, then go back in a week or so. [*She looks at* **Harold.**]

Harold: Then you'll come. Your ticket won't be no problem; I've got connections.

Beverly: Auntie. I should talk with my auntie.

Harold: Checkin time is six-thirty.

Beverly: I'll decide long before then, sir. Maybe I could telephone your house to let you know.

Harold [*Hurriedly*]: No, no! I try and keep business matters away from home as much as possible . . . Tell you what. I'll send a car 'round about six this evening. If you can come, fine. If not, we'll just have to blunder along best way we can. [*Pats* **Beverly** *on the shoulder.*] Remember, I look on you as I would my own daughter. All right?

Beverly *nods and smiles up at him. Blackout.*

ACT THREE

Scene 2. Early afternoon the same day in Merline's frontyard

Merline *is down right, doing her laundry. She shuttles between a washtub and a rinsing tub. The washtub contains a scrub-board and is so placed that* **Merline** *faces the audience. The rinsing tub is parallel to the wings. As she slaps the clothes around in the washtub she sings lugubriously and with obvious pleasure.*

Merline: When the roll is called up yonder,
When the roll is called up yonder,
When the roll is called up yonder,
When the roll is called up yonder,
I'll be there!

On that bright and shining mornin
When the dead in Christ shall rise . . .

Matilda *enters up right, wearing her maid's uniform and carrying a large bag in which are stuffed an assortment of oddments, including a doll, beach-ball, still-wearable woman's dress, tin of soup, pair of girl's shoes, girdles, a loaf of bread, an umbrella, and a package of bologna. She pauses on entering, like a bloodhound sniffing the air, then advances like a latecomer in noisy shoes entering church during silent prayers. With her neck craned forward she resembles a vulture.*

Matilda: Merline! Merline, oh!

Merline *stops singing.*

Merline: *Thought* I hear someone call my name.

Matilda: And you ain' answer 'cause you t'ink it was sperrit and der sperrit would take yer voice, hey? The way you singin sound like somethin good happen.

Merline: What good depend on who it concern. One man cerasie is anodder man poison. Sit down, Matilda. Take the weight off yer legs.

Matilda: I'll be only too willin. [*Sits in the space on the box holding the rinsing tub.*] Talk 'bout tired? Das me. Dem jitney run so unperdictable I haddie walk home. [*Sighs deeply and rubs her leg.*]

Merline: A long soak in a basin o' salt and warm water is all you need and you ready to go again.

Matilda: No more work for me today.

Merline: Dis ain' your knockin-off time; can' be much later dan twelve o'clock.

Matilda: I did wan' come home so bad I plead sick an' Miz Davies take pity and gimme the rest o' the day off.

Merline [*Drying her hands on her dress front in preparation for gossip.*]**:** Das kind of her.

Matilda: Not sayin I wan' be ungrateful or put down Miz Davies or anyt'ing, but I gat ideas regardin that li'l deed o' kindness. [*Pause.*] I t'ink she only too glad to get rid o' me.

Merline: Why?

Matilda [*Taking on an air of conspiracy*]**:** Well, between you and me and the washtub—look like t'ings comin' to a head! You know, in relation to dat li'l matter I tell you 'bout last week. [*Sits back with a self-satisfied smirk.*] But dey can' fool me . . . I see like I don' see and hear like I don' hear, but I know.

Merline: Know what?

Matilda: I know what I know. [*She rummages in her bag, spilling out the various treasures.*]

Merline: Only we two here, Matilda, and dere is no such t'ing as secret between friends . . . Moreover, the people we discussin ain' known to me personal so I can' see why you should play Bo Peep wit' any news you come 'cross . . . What you doin'?

Matilda [*Holding up the dress*]**:** Miz Davies give me dis only dis mornin. Good, hey? [**Merline** *makes an adequate response.*] Pure linen. Jus right for Lodge. [*Plunges into the bag and comes up with the doll.*] Missis gimme dis, too. For my Gertrude. [*Digs up the beach-ball.*] And dis . . . and dis . . . [*and the child's shoes*] and dis . . .

Merline: She eider damn generous or jus plain previous. Ain' Christmas yet.

Matilda: You couldn' be more right . . . I ain' no fool. Dat woman like plenty people who never had nothin and manage to get somethin—she stingy! She will put li'l five dollars in yer Christmas card or give you a ribbon her li'l girls don' want, once in a while, but when she so considerate out of season I know was somethin fishy. I say to myself, I say, "Matilda Bascombe, erry-t'ing that fry ain' lard! Dis woman eider dream Christ comin tomorrow and wan' make her soul right or she tryin to buy you off." Das what I say to myself. And the common sense what was the only t'ing my ma leave me when she pass on—that common sense say dis ain' no makin'-peace-wit-God operation. Dis plain adulterated, amalgamated bribery. And right dere and den I decide to go 'long wit' her. If she wan' buy my silence I ger make her pay good!

Merline: Well, well, well . . . She give you the bread too?

Matilda: No. I stop to the Chinese and get that for lunch. [*Reaches into the bag and draws out a bottle.*] Still and all, some t'ings I don' wait for her to gee me. Whichin she wouldn' anyhow, since she don' believe in spirits. Dis here from Mister Davies—unbeknownst to him, of course.

Merline: Of course. [*Laughs.*] Damn. A whole bottle.

Matilda: Go bring two glasses; let we moisten we tonsils.

Merline [*Turning to go for the glasses.*]**:** When smartness been givin' out, you sure get more dan your share.

Matilda: Der good Lord only promise us two t'ings: a livin' and a killin!

There is general laughter. **Merline** *exits.* **Matilda** *breaks the seal on the bottle and takes a quick swig, then wipes her mouth.*

Matilda: Yes, ma'am, a livin' and a killin!

Merline [*Re-entering with two mismatched glasses and speaking while* **Matilda** *pours the drinks.*]**:** Of course, as you know, I is a woman don' drink. Not me. Last time I touch a drop was when Jennifer christen. [*Takes a sip.*] Though, if t'ings go the way dey goin', might not be long 'fore I get my next taste. [*She pauses mysteriously.* **Matilda** *can scarcely restrain her curiosity.*]

Matilda [*Grabbing hold of* **Merline**'*s skirt and pulling it taut against her stomach insinuatingly*]: More christenin comin up, hey? Lemme be godmother.

Merline [*Laughing*]: Go 'long wid you. I past de age for second spring. Leave that to you young folks . . . No, is Bev'ly.

Were it possible, **Matilda's** *ears would stand up straight, like a dog's.*

Matilda: Oho! And you been tellin me nothin comin of her an' dat Haitian feller affair.

Merline: He ain' no Haitian. Much as I hate he guts he Bahamian.

Matilda: Be he whatsoever he is, somethin come of it for sure. . . . My invitation still stand. . . to be godmother. Tell Bev'ly dat.

Merline: If you wasn' my friend, Matilda, I would swear you gat a vicious mind what delight in scandal. I never tell you Bev'ly pregnant.

Matilda: You say you soon taste more rum.

Merline: And you jump to conclusion. I was talkin' 'bout weddin, dammit, not no fool christenin. The cart before der horse.

Matilda [*Exhaling a long sigh*]: O-o-o-o-h! It finally come to that, hey? When der weddin ger be?

Merline: Dey settlin' dat tonight. [*Looks grave.*] However dey decide, you know who goin' be busy. Me. I suppose I will gattie act as mother-giver.

Matilda: Father-giver.

Merline: What?

Matilda: Is father-giver. Someone to give 'way the bride if it transpire her pa can' be dere. Next of kin in the male line have to stand in.

Merline: Dat rule me out, den. I don' much mind. Givin' Bev'ly 'way to dat sly young man is not my idea of parent-like duty. If must be, must be, but I don' wan' no hand in it. [*Takes a sip of the rum.*]

Matilda: What you gat 'gainst him so?

Merline: He look slippery . . . and he put on too extry for someone in his station . . . Den he mouth hard. If I had mind to, I could tell you things.

Matilda: Who stop you?

Merline: Only me one talkin. You never say what else it was 'bout dem Davies people—aside from the eldest gal bein' big . . . If I could talk fam'ly business, you mussie could talk 'bout raw strangers . . . Well?

Matilda: Well . . . same t'ing dere. Seem like der boy goin' make a honest woman outta Sonia.

Merline: I glad to hear dat. Like I always say, if he could drop he load, he mussie could pick up hers.

Matilda: Couldn' 'gree wid yer more. Anyway, the youngest Davies child tell me say der boy been round dere with Sonia after class Friday night and meet with the mister and mistress. We both know what dat pretends. [*Gives* **Merline** *a meaningful look and sings*]:

Here comes the bride,
Here comes the bride,
Here comes the bride,
For to be married today!

Pity I wasn' dere to gather more detail—though I t'ink der child say the boy name was . . . [*Seeming to consider*] I ain' too sharp on names, but I sure it was . . . lemme see. . . . Was . . . Well, I'll be a monkey's uncle; das gatta be it! I certain sure das it. Well, goes to show—when it rain it pour . . .

Merline: What you mumblin 'bout? Say he name if you goin' say it; don' matter to me. [*Silence.*] Awright, if you don' wan' say it you don' have to. Since is police secret.

Matilda: You wouldn' mind hearin? Of course, could be coincidence.

Merline: [*Suspicious and annoyed*] You can' be wan' say it was . . .

Matilda: Lionel. At least das what I t'ink she say it was.

Merline *looks stricken. She hurries to the washtub, turns her back on* **Matilda**, *and picks up an article of clothing, which she merely holds in her hand.* **Matilda** *notes* **Merline**'*s perturbation, not without malice.*

Matilda: Of course I could be wrong. She might even mean some odder Lionel. After all, I didn' see him. One t'ing I don' like 'bout small community—errybody gat der same name. [*Roots in her bag and comes up with the bologna, opens the package and takes out a slice.*] Hungriness whippin my insides. Want piece, Merline?

Merline: No, t'anks, Matilda, no t'anks. When I busy like dis my stomach does refuse food. [*She pauses and turns to* **Matilda** *almost against her will.*] So der young man name Lion-el. [*Laughs.*] Would be funny if the two couples get married same day . . . They wouldn' have the same surname, though. [*Laughs.*] Das for sure.

Matilda [*Rising to the bait*]: You right dere. Joseph ain' common.

Merline: Yeah. The title Joseph ain' common. [*She wrings out an article of clothing absent-mindedly and takes it to the rinsing tub.* **Matilda** *notices this abstraction.*]

Matilda: You ain' scrub dat.

Merline: It wasn't dirty. [*She concentrates on swishing the clothes around in the rinsing tub.* **Matilda** *leaps up and crosses left.*]

Matilda: Look like I in der way . . . [*She laughs self-consciously.*] Well, time for me to be goin'. You know, I walk straight past my own house where I did wan' see you so bad. Is nice to have friends to talk to—even if is only 'bout strange people business . . . I goin' now . . . You could send back der iron board wit' Jennifer when yer ready.

Matilda *goes out the way she came in.* **Merline** *pauses a few seconds at the rinsing tub.*

Merline: No, is just suspicious-mindedness. Like Bev'ly say, maybe I attack him too much. But is too strange to be accident. And deep down within instinct tell me that boy up to no good—like a lot of dem foreign mixture. Can' trust em. Can' trust em no further than you can spit.

Merline *wrings out some articles of clothing violently, places them in the face basin, and heaves the basin against her right hip. She goes out down right. Lights fade to the count of five.*

ACT THREE

Scene 3. Late that same afternoon in Merline's frontyard

Sound of radio soap opera up loud. Lights up on **Merline** *dressed as in Scene 1, clearing away washing material.* **Jennifer** *enters wearing school uniform.*

Merline [*Passing scrub-board to* **Jennifer**]**:** Lean this up in the back to dry; then come help me with these tubs.

Jennifer *goes off with the board and returns quickly. She grips one handle of the rinsing tub while* **Merline** *grips the other. They carry the tub offstage. They repeat this procedure with the washtub and return.*

Merline: Okay; go change dem clothes. You too like prance 'round in good t'ings.

Jennifer *scampers into the house. While* **Merline** *is out of sight putting away the rinsing-tub crate* **Beverly** *enters down right with her handbag and manila envelope. She goes into the house tossing her belongings on to the sofa and turns off the radio.* **Merline** *hears the silence and returns.*

Merline: So you come. You mussie get job, you been gone so long.

Beverly: Yes, I did.

Merline: Well, how the first day was?

Beverly: Strange and mixed up. For one thing, Lionel turned up commanding me to leave. And I just got the job, mind.

Merline: Das him all over—bossy! He say why you should leave?

Beverly: Something about the Davies family setting a trap.

Merline: Davies. Das they title, hey?

Beverly [*Sitting*]**:** Uh huh. Seem like he knows Mr. Davies' daughter, Sonia, and was scared I would find out. Not that there was much to find out. [*She goes through the back curtains with her handbag and envelope and returns without them.*]

Merline: That so?

Beverly: Uh huh.

Merline: Dis Sonia. What she like?

Beverly: In Mr. Davies' words, "friendly as a child." An easy person for a man to strike up a casual relationship with, but no need to worry: she isn't pretty at all.

Merline: When you gat money you don' need looks.

Beverly: So you say. Anyway, I came to get ready. Mr. Davies invited me on a business trip and the car's coming 'round about six o'clock.

Merline: Well kiss my eye! What kinda business trip dis, so rush-rush?

Beverly: To settle a deal in Miami. Won't take long.

Merline: No self-respectin' young girl would go off with no married man, business or not. You better set right here and find something to do what could profit yer mind. Read book or something.

Beverly: You called my books trash.

Merline: Still, I rather see you *readin* trash before my face than t'ink o' you *doin'* trash in my absence.

Beverly: There you go again, same suspicious mind . . . This is a business trip. You've been behind me all the while, throwing jeers and talking 'bout how things tough and I'd better find a job. Now I have a job all you want to do is spoil my chances. This is the best chance I ever had, and I am taking it!

Merline: Hard-head bird don' make good soup!

Beverly: Besides, in Miami I'll get to look for a wedding dress.

Merline: You mightn' need none.

Beverly *jerks out of her reverie and reverts to the sulky behaviour that* **Merline***'s mistrust usually evokes.*

Beverly: Says who?

Merline: Not if what I hear is true.

Beverly [*Curious, in spite of herself*]: What old story you trotting out now?

Merline: Matilda right.

Beverly: Matilda?

Merline: She say look like the Davies woman tryin to buy her silence. Look like they buying you, too.

Beverly: Buy me? Wait a minute . . . What does nosy Matilda have to do with the Davies family?

Merline: She's dey maid. Remember when me and her been to Lodge she tell me 'bout der people she workin for? Well, seem like the oldest gal-child pregnant. Anyway, she lucky—her pa gat money so der feller offer marriage. We so, somethin like dat happen, we can' do nothing. Like I say, dat gal lucky. She ger get married and live happy ever after. Finish night school and all, I guess.

Beverly: I don't see what this has to do with me. So Sonia is getting married. Good for her.

Merline [*Wearily*]: Yeah, good—for her.

There is a long silence.

Merline: Accordin to what one of the children tell Matilda, was a meetin after class Friday gone—between Mr. Davies and der feller. To make final plans.
Beverly: I still don't see what this has to do with me.

There is a pause.

Merline: It ain' de end o' der world.

The women stare at each other. **Beverly** *breaks away, goes out and returns with a suitcase and armful of clothes. She throws the suitcase onto the settee and deliberately begins to pack the clothes.*

Merline: Where you goin'?
Beverly: Ask a stupid question . . .
Merline: None o' your sassy, now.

Lionel *enters down right, comes to the front steps and looks in.*

Lionel: Afternoon, Mrs. Evans. Hi, Bev.
Merline: Hmmph!

Merline *marches behind the curtains.* **Lionel** *looks at* **Beverly,** *who ignores him and continues packing.*

Lionel: Bev, don't keep being vexed. I can explain.
Beverly: What's there to explain?
Lionel: About Sonia and me . . . There's nothing between us, Bev. Never was.

Beverly: Why you think I feel there's something between you? You work for her daddy; you had to meet sometime. [**Lionel** *heaves a sigh of relief.*] But you didn't have to make a habit of it.

Lionel [*Caught unawares*]: What?

Beverly: You didn't have to make a habit of meeting her. Going to all that trouble of starting night classes just to be with her. And you could have shown more taste—at least waited till the sweat you worked up with me dried before you ran to her. Stud!

Lionel: That's what you believe? That I signed up for classes to get next to Sonia? You really think our meeting Friday night had something behind it? I suppose it wouldn't do any good saying I went to classes to get further along. For Christ sake, Bev, I just met Sonia that morning!

Beverly: You must have worked fast.

Lionel: What's that supposed to mean?

Beverly: Come, Lionel, do better than that. You think I was born big as I am? You meet a girl for the first time that morning and by night you're talking over wedding plans with her father?

Lionel *collapses onto the settee.* **Beverly** *interprets this as a sign of guilt.*

Lionel: You seem to have knowledgeable sources. Davies been filling your ears with smooth lies? I *told* you to leave. He was setting a trap, Bev.

Beverly: For you or me?

Lionel: Both. But it failed to work on me. Bev, let me tell you how this Sonia story goes.

Beverly *turns away, clicks the suitcase shut, then stands it by the door.*

Beverly: I don't want to hear any more of your lies or excuses. [*Mimicking*] "We can't get married for at least three weeks . . . "

Lionel: That's true! Ask any minister.

Beverly: And to top it off, I must leave the very job that could give us a start! . . . Lionel . . . Lionel, look at me. Do I seem that stupid? Why don't you admit you wanted me to leave because of fear I'd find out about you and Sonia? About your arrangement?

Lionel: You read too many silly love books. I wish you'd get it through your thick skull that there is no "arrangement" between Sonia and me.

Beverly: So now I'm thick-skulled.

Lionel: And an ass.

Beverly: Takes one to find one.

Lionel: This is childish. When you're this way it's senseless trying to talk to you. I'll come back after you sort out your mind. [*Looking at the suitcase by the entrance*] A trip to the island should do you good. Your mother might penetrate that shell.

Beverly: You really think I'm running off to some corner to pine, don't you? That's where you're wrong. I'm going to Miami on business, and I don't want to see you around when I get back. Give my regards to the baby.

Lionel: What the hell you talking 'bout?

Beverly: What I learned from my "knowledgeable source." Oh, it's all right. Go ahead and say it's a shotgun affair. I'm fool enough to believe that, you know. Tell me you hate marrying money. I can see you crying all the way to the bank.

Lionel *rises from the settee and grabs* **Beverly** *by her shoulders.*

Lionel: I did not make Sonia pregnant.
Beverly: That's been said before.

Jennifer *runs in.*

Jennifer: Bev! Bev! Car out there to you!
Beverly: Let me go, Lionel!
Lionel: Not until you listen!

Jennifer *dances up and down urgently.*

Jennifer: Hurry, Bev. The driver say if you comin' or not.
Lionel: Sonia's pregnant by someone else, not by me.

Merline *enters from behind the curtains and stands watching the trio, cutlass in hand.*

Beverly: Let me go!
Lionel: No!
Merline: You better do like she say 'fore I separate your ass from your elbow.

Merline *advances ominously.* **Lionel** *Lets* **Beverly** *go, more from the hopelessness of the situation than from fear of* **Merline**.

Beverly [*To* **Jennifer**]: Tell the driver I'm coming.

Jennifer *darts off, downstage.* **Beverly** *picks up the suitcase and moves towards the front steps.* **Lionel** *strides in her direction and tries to touch her.*

Beverly: Keep away from me. I'm through with you. Marry your Sonia—I don't care. I can make it on my own. I don't need you!

Lionel: Please, Bev, just one minute.

Beverly *wavers for a moment.* **Lionel** *holds her hand. For that moment she is undecided; then pride wins and she pulls away.*

Beverly: I mean it. Leave me alone, you no-good, two-timing, double-crossing, scrawny-necked, piss-tailed, low-down Haitian freak!

Lionel *releases her and draws away.*

Lionel: You must be off your head.

Beverly: No, sweety-pie. I'm *on* my head, and that's just where I'll stay. Go with Sonia. That won't stop you from being the nothing you always were . . . just like your pa and those other generations of rock-pickers!

Beverly *rushes off, downstage.* **Lionel** *turns to* **Merline**.

Lionel: She's got it all wrong.

Merline *eyes* **Lionel** *unlovingly.*

Merline: Don' tell me.

Lionel: I have to tell someone . . . Mr. Davies' daughter got pregnant by a married politician and he wants me to marry her and give the child a name. Then he made me look guilty today in front of Bev when I went to warn her.

Merline: Simple so? Well, why you ain' come right out and tell Bev'ly instead o' beatin round the bush?

Lionel: Her mind was poisoned against me. It's hard to reason with her.

Merline: Anyway, dey say where there's life, there's hope.

When Bev'ly come back from dat trip with Mr. Davies I ger talk to her, put her straight.

Lionel: What you say?

Merline: You shell-shocked, aye? I say . . .

Lionel: *Beverly* went on a trip with Mr. Davies?

Merline: Yeah, to Miami . . . What happen? You don' trust her? [*Pauses. No response.*] Somethin wrong? [*No response.*] Shucks, I can' bother wit yinna. Do as you please.

Merline *goes out behind the curtain.*

Lionel *descends the steps and stands in the frontyard, downstage centre.*

Lionel: So who was the sucker, aye, Lionel, my boy? Who was the fall guy? Hmm? There you were fighting them off on all sides and she gives in without a struggle. Ready and willing. Must have been a record for him . . . What she say? "You're nothing"? That's a joke. Before moneybags Davies came along I was *plenty*. Old string-along Lionel . . . But then she found a better deal, so what does she do? Grabs the first lie she could latch on to; then snip-snap, no more String-along Lionel. And she says *I've* sold out! Off she goes with the prince of prostitutes and *I'm* the one who sold out . . . But I'll show her; I'll show all of them. "No-good, double-crossing Haitian freak," hey? I'll really freak you out. Freak all of you out . . . How? Metal? [*Thinks.*] No, that's too easy. No, make them squirm. Do it from the inside; that's the way. Break them from within . . . [*Laughs.*] Make living dead out of them. [*Laughs*] Boss of the living dead. Me. [*Laughs.*]

Lionel *races off, down right. Blackout. Telephone rings in*

Davies living room. Spot on **Lionel**, *forestage right. Spot on Davies telephone table. Ringing continues.* **Erma** *enters and picks up the telephone.*

Erma: Hello.

Lionel: Hello. Mrs. Davies?

Erma: Yes. Who is speaking, please?

Lionel: Lionel Joseph.

Erma: Joseph?

Lionel: Yes. You know, as in Mary and Joseph.

Erma: I see. What can I do for you, Mr. Joseph?

Lionel: It's like this. Mr. Davies and I were discussing a little proposition . . .

Erma: Yes?

Lionel: . . . and I was supposed to turn in my answer today.

Erma: Oh. You turn in your answer yet, Mr. Joseph?

Lionel: No. That's what I'm calling about . . . You know, Mrs. Davies, I don't quite go with discussing business over the phone. May I come over to see you?

Erma: When?

Lionel: Why, n-o-w, Mrs. Davies. If you have the time.

Erma: But Sonia isn't here, and Mr. Davies has gone out. Away.

Lionel: I hear you're a fine cook, Mrs. Davies.

Erma [*Warming to the compliment*]: Would you like to come round to supper, Mr. Joseph?

Lionel: Lionel.

Erma: By all means, Lionel.

Blackout. Sound of children clapping and singing.

Children:

Clap clap clap clap
Clap clap clap clap

Clap clap clap clap
Clap clap clap clap

Blue Hill water dry;
No way to wash my clothes.
I remember the Saturday night,
Boiled fish and johnny cake.

(*Chant*) Man take one and satisfy;
Woman take two and make a moo!
Man take one and satisfy;
Woman take two and make a moo!

Chant and song continue to lights-up. **Merline** *enters her front room, goes to the door to track down the ring-play source, finds the frontyard empty, descends the steps, faces upstage, arms akimbo, and emits a powerful yell.*

Merline: Jenn-er-fer!

Jennifer *appears in the frontyard and walks cautiously up to* **Merline. Merline** *turns to face* **Jennifer**. *Tense silence.* **Merline** *reaches out and draws* **Jennifer** *to her chest in an embrace. Lights out.*

For the late Carlton E. Francis, former headmaster of
Southern Senior School, New Providence, Bahamas

Macmillan Education
Between Towns Road, Oxford OX4 3PP
A division of Macmillan Publishers Limited
Companies and representatives throughout the world

www.macmillan-caribbean.com

ISBN 978-0-333-63706-7

First published 1987

Cover Illustration based on an original drawing by James O.Rolle

Printed and bound in Malaysia

2016 2015 2014 2013 2012
19 18